# SHOWERS OF BLESSINGS

Herschel H. Hobbs

Baker Book House
Grand Rapids, Michigan

Copyright © 1973 by
Baker Book House Company

ISBN: 0-8010-4070-1

Library of Congress Catalog
Card Number: 72-97560
Printed in the United States of America

Dedicated to
HIM
who enables us to "trace the
rainbow thro' the rain."

# Contents

1 **THE HIGHER BLESSEDNESS** ....... 11
   Blessed ........................ 13
   Blessed, the Poor ................ 16
   Blessed, the Mournful ............ 19
   Blessed, the Meek ............... 23
   Blessed, the Hungry and Thirsty .... 26
   Blessed, the Merciful ............ 30
   Blessed, the Pure in Heart ........ 33
   Blessed, the Peacemakers ......... 36
   Blessed, the Persecuted .......... 39
   The Greater Blessedness ......... 42

2 **AMID LIFE'S CERTAINTIES** ....... 45
   The Bible ...................... 47
   Our Heavenly Father ............. 51
   Our Elder Brother ............... 54
   Our Divine Helper ............... 58
   The Greatest Love ............... 62
   God's Providence ................ 65
   Peace .......................... 68
   Chastisement ................... 71
   Health Is ...................... 75
   A Godly Home .................. 79

3 **LIFE'S "COOL SEQUESTER'D" WAY** 83
   On Being a Blessing ............. 85
   The Joy of Living ............... 88

## CONTENTS

Pass It On! .......................... 91
Owned or Owner? .................. 94
Blessings in Disguise .............. 96
Joy in Tribulation ................. 99
The Blessing of Humility .......... 101
The Virtue of Patience ........... 104
Contentment .................... 107
Faith ........................... 110
Hope ........................... 114
Love ........................... 117
Growing Lovely, Growing Old ...... 121

# Introduction

Flowers are lovely; love is flower-like;
Friendship is a sheltering tree;
Oh, the joys that came down shower-like;
Of friendship, love, and liberty.
Samuel Taylor Coleridge

Those who have lived any appreciable portion of life know that blessings come in many guises. They may come clothed in the splendor of sunshine. Or they may wear the darksome hue of rain. But through eyes of faith you may see God's hand in the cloud as well as in the rainbow. Indeed, were there no cloud there would be no rainbow. As the Arabs observe, all sunshine makes a desert. And if there were no clouds we would curse the sun. A fulfilled life calls for sunshine as well as rain. And there are blessings in both if only we will see them.

Happy is the soul that by God's grace can "trace the rainbow thro' the rain." For in the words of Sarah Flower Adams:

He sendeth sun, he sendeth shower,
  Alike they're needful for the flower;

> And joy and tears alike are sent
> > To give the soul fit nourishment.
> As comes to me or cloud or sun,
> > Father! thy will, not mine, be done.

Percy Bysshe Shelley echoes this same thought when in "The Cloud" he says, "I bring fresh showers for the thirsting flowers."

So whether you tread a path strewn with the sun's rays or with the cloud's raindrops, life can be a thing of beauty and blessing. For as one has said, beauty is in the eyes—and we may add, the heart—of the beholder.

So often we remember the blights of life more than its blessings. But when the sum of life is taken, the latter far exceed the former. And even the fabric of blight contains the golden threads of God's blessings, if we have eyes to see.

Several years ago it was my privilege to write a little book titled *When the Rain Falls*. The testimony of many speaks of the blessings and strength derived from musing over its pages. This has led me to write of the silvery lining that is behind every cloud, to point out that for those who believe, there are blessings untold in the many-colored experiences of life.

One is fond of plucking flowers along the rose scattered path. But he should never forget that they are the blessings of the showers. And as one looks heavenward, behind each frowning face he may see a smiling Providence.

> May never was the month of love,
> For May is full of flowers;
> But rather April, wet by kind,
> For love is full of showers.
>
> Robert Southwell

Praise God, from whom all blessings flow!
Thomas Ken

# THE HIGHER BLESSEDNESS

# Blessed

*"And he opened his mouth, and taught them, saying, Blessed. . . ."*—Matt. 5:2-3a

These are the opening words of the Beatitudes, and are used by Jesus to introduce His Sermon on the Mount. Matthew's Gospel presents Jesus as the King. He was "born King of the Jews" (Matt. 2:2). Note that He did not *become* King; He was *born* King.

The Sermon on the Mount has been called "The Manifesto of the King." I prefer to call it "The Constitution of the Kingdom of God." It may be outlined as (1) The citizens of the kingdom (chap. 5); (2) The values in the kingdom (chap. 6); and (3) The relationships within the kingdom (chap. 7). Our present purpose is to see the quality that characterizes these citizens. Jesus summed it up in one word: *blessed.* This word does not necessarily describe the Christian's feeling within himself, although this cannot be ignored entirely. But the primary thought involved is the state of the Christian as seen by Jesus. He described it as a state of blessedness.

Some interpreters see Jesus as giving nine beatitudes, but I prefer to regard the number as eight. What some consider as eight and nine (Matt. 5:10-12) actually deal with one idea. But more to the point, if you examine Matthew 5:3-11 you will note that in verses 3-10 (King James Version) *are* is in italics, showing that this verb is not in the original Greek text. In verse 11 *are* is not italicized, which means that it is in the Greek text. It is for this reason that I regard verses 10-12 as one beatitude.

How may we understand the word *blessed?* The Greek word is *makarioi* (plural), from *makarios* (singular). It is difficult to translate this word into brief, smooth English. Some translate it as "happy." Since it is in the form of an interjection it is rendered "Oh, the happiness of." However, "happy" is limited in its meaning. It suggests the word *happening;* that is, a condition which is dependent on what happens to you. If it is something you regard as good, then you are happy. If it is bad, then you are unhappy. Jesus was not saying that the Christian's condition depends on what is happening to him. To the contrary, He said that regardless of outward circumstances the Christian is "blessed." It is a state that is governed by an inward, not an outward, circumstance.

To more than any other, I am indebted to William Barclay in understanding this word. In his little book on Matthew he points out that the feminine form of this Greek word *(hē makaria)* was used to describe the island of Cyprus as "The Happy Isle." It was said that Cyprus was so beautiful, fertile, and rich in water and other natural resources that one could live on this island all his life, never leaving it, and yet find on it all that was necessary for him to live a rich, full life.

In this sense Jesus was saying that in Him the Christian

possesses all that is necessary to live a full, complete life. The Christian is not *self-sufficient* but *Christ-sufficient.* So that "blessed" is suggestive of Jesus' words, "My peace I give unto you" (John 14:27).

Since this word is used without a verb, it is what may be called an *absolute.* It is an unchangeable condition. Whether you as a Christian are in a storm or in a calm, you are "blessed."

As we will see, these beatitudes form a progression of ideas. Thus they do not describe eight different types of people, but rather describe one person in a succession of experiences. Indeed, they run the entire gamut of your spiritual life. The first four deal with the Christian's relation to God; the last four treat his relation to men.

If this brief discussion seems to be somewhat technical, it is for a purpose. That purpose is to enable you better to understand the state of blessedness which Jesus designs for His people.

If some of these states seem to be peculiar, you should remember that Christ's people are a peculiar people. Not odd, but different from people of the world. They enjoy a different relationship to God, to each other, and to the world. Worldly values differ from heavenly values (Matt. 6). And the Christian should look away from mere worldly happiness to the joy and peace that only Christ can give. It is thus, and only thus, that you can truly be called "blessed" in the deepest sense of the word.

# Blessed, the Poor

*"Blessed are the poor in spirit: for theirs is the kingdom of heaven."*—Matt. 5:3

Jesus was fond of teaching by paradox. A paradox is a statement which on the surface seems to be self-contradictory. It is this very contrast that enables us to remember many of Jesus' teachings. They stab our memory, and shock us into understanding as we look beyond or beneath the surface meaning to grasp the truth involved in the statement. For instance, Jesus taught that you possess by giving, you save by losing. By earth's standards these seem to be contradictory statements. However, when applied to life's deepest experiences, their truth is evident.

To Jesus' listeners "Blessed, the poor" was strange to their ears. For among the ancient Jews wealth was regarded as a blessing and poverty as a curse. Wealth was thought to be an evidence of God's favor while poverty was a sign of His judgment. Of course, James (2:5; 5:1) identified wealth with wickedness and poverty with piety. But while the Book of James is the most Jewish of the New Testament writings, it still reflects the Christian ethical standard. So to the average Jew of that day it would have seemed more likely for Jesus to say, "Blessed, the rich." Instead, He said, "Blessed, the poor."

However, He did not stop there. He said, "Blessed, the poor in spirit." Thus He lifted the idea out of the mundane into the spiritual.

The word translated "poor" means abject poverty. Another word so rendered meant a working man who provided for his own needs, but with nothing left over. But the word used here means absolute poverty. It was used of the beggar Lazarus (Luke 16:20), who was absolutely dependent on others for the bare necessities of life. Also it was used of the widow who gave her two mites (Mark 12:42-43). In this case it could mean one who worked for a living but in addition had to beg in order to supplement her earnings for life's necessities. However, in either case the poor of whom Jesus spoke were those in abject poverty and who were dependent on others for a living.

Note, however, that Jesus spoke of the "poor in spirit." There is no virtue or vice in either poverty or wealth as such in the material sense. It depends on how one uses it. But in the spiritual sense it is quite a different matter. One who feels that he is rich or self-sufficient in spiritual things is poor indeed. Jesus said that you must recognize and accept your spiritual poverty before you can know true riches.

One who is poor in spirit recognizes his absolute poverty in spiritual matters. As such you will lack the self-sufficiency of the Pharisee (Luke 18:11-12). Contrariwise, you will know that within yourself there is no merit or virtue which recommends you to God. Like the publican, you will not compare yourself with others. You do not parade your virtues before God, but see yourself as totally lacking in His righteousness. Thus you will cry out to God for mercy (Luke 18:13).

In this sense "poor in spirit" corresponds to what theologians call "conviction of sin." You recognize that you are a sinner separated from God. Nevertheless you desire to be more than you are. At the same time you know that you can do nothing about it in your own power. It must be done for you by someone else. As you pray to God you ask for the gift of grace, not for justice. Grace means that God does for you what neither you nor anyone else can do for you. Thus you recognize that your hope lies not in self-sufficiency, but in Christ-sufficiency. Only He can give to you the state of blessedness by which you can live the abundant life.

Thus it is that the poor in spirit are blessed. For only as you have that attitude can you hope to enter into the kingdom of God.

# Blessed, the Mournful

*"Blessed are they that mourn: for they shall be comforted."*—Matt. 5:4

Again Jesus spoke a paradox. For the world regards mourning as anything but blessed. Rather, it says, "Blessed are the happy." Friends offer you their comfort in your sorrows, not in your joys.

The word for "mourn" means to mourn for the dead. It is the strongest word for mourning in the Greek language. The Septuagint, Greek translation of the Old Testament, uses this word for Jacob's mourning when he thought his favorite son, Joseph, was dead (Gen. 37:34).

In the human sense mourning is not blessed. Many kinds of sorrow find no comfort. Certainly the ungodly person sorrows without hope in bereavement (I Thess. 4:13). But for the Christian, even mourning for the dead has rays of hope. You can find comfort in Christ now (Luke 4:18), and the "blessed hope" of the Lord's return is ever in your heart. Then all sorrows will pass away and all tears will be dried.

Wrongs will be righted, and the suffering ones will be justified. It was this blessed hope to which Paul referred when he said, "Wherefore comfort one another with these words" (I Thess. 4:13-18).

For the Christian, mourning in this life may be a blessed thing. Recall the proverb, "All sunshine and no rain produces a desert." In the words of Henry Van Dyke:

> If all life were sunshine,
>   Our faces would be fain
> To feel once more upon them
>   The cooling splash of rain.

All of these things are true. But while they may have been in the background of Jesus' mind, were they primary in His words "Blessed are they that mourn"? If, as I have suggested, the Beatitudes present a progression of experiences, must we not look more deeply to find His specific meaning? Does not the idea of "poor in spirit" carry over into this beatitude? As one who possesses no power within yourself to recommend you to God, you are spiritually dead outside of Christ. It is one thing to recognize your sinful condition, it is another to mourn because of it. Simply to recognize one's unworthiness may drive a person even more deeply into sin.

So Jesus evidently was saying that for you to be blessed in this lack of spiritual self-sufficiency you must be brought to mourn as to your abiding in spiritual death (Eph. 2:1). Recognizing your own sinfulness and unworthiness, you must be plunged into deep mourning as for the dead. You mourn not only because of what your sin has done to you, but even more significantly, because of what it has done to God.

You may be sorry for your sins—sorry or filled with regret

because others have discovered them. Or because you must suffer the consequences of them. A man in prison may experience such sorrow. But if his sorrow goes no further, he will probably continue in crime after serving his sentence.

In the truest sense Jesus was talking about *repentance* from sin. The Greek language has two words that are translated "repent" in the New Testament. One of these words means *regret.* It was used of Judas in Matthew 27:3. He regretted his sin of betrayal, but he had no change of heart. Therefore, he went out and committed suicide. The other word means a change of heart, mind, attitude, or the entire direction of one's life. While not used in the context, Peter experienced this repentance of his sin of denial and became a powerful servant for Christ.

The difference between these words is clearly seen in II Corinthians 7:9-10. "Now I rejoice not that ye were made sorry, but that ye sorrowed to repentance [change of heart, mind, and attitude]: for ye were made sorry after a godly manner...for godly sorrow worketh repentance [same as above] to salvation not to be repented of [or regretted, same as in Matt. 27:3]: but the sorrow of the world worketh death."

So to mourn as dead in sin is to experience godly sorrow, which leads you to true repentance. Thus it is that conviction of sin should be followed by repentance from sin. It is such an experience that produces the state of blessedness of which Jesus spoke.

Those who experience true repentance "shall be comforted." The word rendered thus is like the word rendered "Comforter" in John 14:6. So if you mourn in godly sorrow, you will know the comfort of the Holy Spirit. He produces both conviction and repentance. He convicts of sin (John 16:7-11). And in the seeking heart He brings repentance from sin.

In such a condition you as a lost sinner know that you are not alone in dealing with your sin problem. You have the divine Helper who points you away from sin to the Savior.

In this way you can be blessed as you are led to reject self-sufficiency for Christ-sufficiency. In this sense "blessed are they that mourn: for they shall be comforted."

# Blessed, the Meek

*"Blessed are the meek: for they shall inherit the earth."*—Matt. 5:5

It is unfortunate that the English word *meek* suggests *weak*. It connotes one who is weak or cowardly. Such a meek person is seen as one who endures but does not strike back or strive. He merely sits and waits.

But the Greek word so translated is a strong, noble one. While the world even in that day despised the meek, Jesus elevated its meaning to noble heights. In doing so He uttered another paradox.

The world then and now sees the mighty inheriting the earth. They run over the meek in order to gain their wordly aims. But by contrast Jesus said that the meek shall inherit the land.

How, then, may we understand "the meek"? A meek person is one who recognizes his shortcomings (v. 3), is free from pride, and is filled with humility (v. 4). He realizes that he is not sufficient within himself; so he is willing to submit to someone else who can supply his lack. The resultant meaning is that he is teachable. Thus he is willing to enroll as a disciple under a teacher.

Someone else stated it in another way. A meek person is one who under life's pressures has learned to bend his will, setting aside his own notions as he stands in awe before the greatness and grace of God. Such are characterized by humble trust rather than self-will or arrogant independence. The self-asserting and self-trusting may think that they possess the earth. But in the perspective of eternity and eternal values, it is the meek—or as someone has called them, "the terrible meek"—who really inherit the land.

When seen in its context, what did Jesus mean by "the meek"? Was He not speaking of those who exercise faith in Him? Conviction and repentance must be followed by faith if you are to be saved. Recognizing your lack of self-sufficiency (conviction), and mourning for your sins (repentance), you turn to Christ in faith or commitment. Without this commitment, conviction is meaningless and repentance is nothing more than regret.

Regarding the meek as those who are teachable, Jesus' words in Matthew 11:28-30 throw light on this matter. To "take one's yoke" meant to enroll under a teacher. So Jesus invited those who labored and were heavy laden to become His pupils or disciples. Such was an act of faith (trust, commitment) in the Teacher. The figure of becoming Jesus' disciple is akin to His figure of the new birth (John 3:3).

Here you see the sequence: conviction, repentance, faith. When you in faith commit yourself to Christ you bend your will to His. You admit that you need teaching and are teachable. By the power of the Holy Spirit you enter into this state of Christ-sufficiency. In Him you find all that is necessary to live a full, complete life. Thus you are "blessed."

So it is that you "inherit the earth." The word rendered "earth" means *the land.* Not simply the land of Palestine. But in the larger sense it suggests the kingdom of God (v. 3). For you to be a citizen in the King's realm you must experience conviction, repentance, and faith.

Having done so, as Paul says, you become God's child, or heir of God and a joint-heir with Jesus Christ (Rom. 8:17). The apostle used this promise in connection with his figure of adoption, a Roman custom that Paul likened to the new birth. A man could go through the process of adopting a son, usually a slave. In this ceremony he paid all obligations against the slave and assumed all of his future obligations. In turn, the adopted son assumed the responsibilities of sonship. He was regarded as being born again into a new family. And he became a joint-heir along with naturally born sons of all that his new father possessed. The adopting ceremony was done in the presence of witnesses. In the Christian experience corresponding to this Roman legal transaction, the Holy Spirit is the witness (see Gal. 4:6-7).

So, dear friend, as a teachable one you are "blessed" as in faith you inherit the "land" or God's kingdom through faith in Jesus Christ. Nevermore must you rely on your own self-sufficiency, but on the sufficiency that is in God in Christ. In Him you possess all that is necessary to live a full, complete life. It is in this sense that Jesus could exclaim, "Oh, the happiness of the meek: for they shall inherit the kingdom of heaven!"

# Blessed, the Hungry and Thirsty

*"Blessed are they which do hunger and thirst after righteousness: for they shall be filled."*—Matt. 5:6

Frank Stagg reminds us that this beatitude did not arise among people whose problem was overweight. Indeed, it is difficult for us to understand it fully where food is abundant and water is available in the home simply by the turning of a tap. If you would appreciate it fully you must see the bloated stomachs of starving children and visit lands where water is at a premium. Jesus lived in a land where water was scarce and food was hard to produce, so His words had a vivid meaning for His hearers. For years I had heard the ballad—

> All day I've faced the barren waste
>   Without a trace of water;
> Cool, clear water.

But I did not really appreciate it until I traveled through the western desert lands of the United States.

Hunger and thirst are two of our most demanding appetites. Physically speaking you would be hard put to find blessedness in such conditions. And yet even these difficulties may become blessings if they cause us to recognize God as the source of each and that we are dependent on Him for food and drink.

However, Jesus went beyond these physical realities to see the spiritual needs of the Christian. He spoke of those who hunger and thirst after righteousness. As the body craves food and drink, and delights in both, the soul of the Christian should crave and delight in righteousness.

The Bible speaks of righteousness in three ways: that which God is in His nature; that which He demands in man, but which man in his own power cannot achieve; that which God bestows on those who believe in His Son as Savior.

If we follow the idea of progression in the Beatitudes, we see in this verse an individual who through conviction, repentance, and faith has received God's righteousness in Christ. This means that God has declared him to be righteous. The word translated "righteousness" belongs to a family of words which means that a condition is not necessarily so, but that one chooses to regard it as being true. So although we are unrighteous, in Christ God chooses to regard us as righteous or justified in His sight.

So as a Christian putting yourself in this verse, you possess God's righteousness in Christ. And as a Christian you continue to hunger and thirst after righteousness. The unsaved person knows no such appetites. But for the one who has been justified before God, the desire for personal righteousness becomes the most craving of appetites. It possesses your very soul. You delight in righteousness within yourself, and yearn for all men to have it. You long to see right triumph over wrong.

But there is more. The figures of the new birth and of

becoming a pupil of Christ both imply a continuing process of growth in your Christian experience. The presence of healthy life in a body makes it to want to grow. One with a taste of knowledge desires more. And when you experience the righteousness which God gives to you in Christ, you want to become more and more like Him. Jesus threw out the challenge when He said, "Be ye therefore perfect, even as your Father which is in heaven is perfect" (Matt. 5:48). As a follower of Jesus you want to be like Him.

I call the condition described in this verse *sanctification*. The word itself means the state of being set apart for God's service. This setting apart was done to you by the Holy Spirit the very second that you received Christ as Savior. The New Testament calls Christians "saints" (I Cor. 1:1), though we do not always act saintly. But we are vessels dedicated to the service of God. As such we should be clean or holy vessels. Sanctification does not come as the climax of a process of ridding ourselves of sin. We are sanctified when our sins are forgiven in Christ. As Jesus sanctified Himself for us in going to the cross as God's means of our redemption (John 17:19), so we are sanctified by the Holy Spirit to do God's will. We are to grow and develop not *into* but *in* the state of being sanctified. In this way we will become vessels better fitted for God's use.

It is this growth which is suggested in our hungering and thirsting after righteousness. As a Christian you should never be satisfied with your present state. You should crave more and more to be maturing into what God intends you to be. Like Paul, you should never feel that you have reached the goal, but should press on (Phil. 3:12-14). Or as Peter says, we must go on growing in grace and in the knowledge of our Lord and Savior Jesus Christ (II Peter 3:18).

The promise is that we "shall be filled." The verb so translated was used of feeding and fattening cattle. So as a kingdom citizen you will be thoroughly satisfied as you attain the purpose for which you receive sustenance from God. Insufficient within yourself alone, you will learn that you can do all things through Christ.

Jesus said that He came that you might have life, and have it "more abundantly" (John 10:10). This means a life so full that it will overflow. And you will bless others by this overflow from your life in Christ. In this manner you will both be blessed and be a blessing. This is the *blessed* life indeed!

In satisfying your hunger and thirst for righteousness, God enables you to become more and more like Christ. But so great is His righteousness that the goal ever exceeds your grasp. Yet you have the promise that when He will appear at the end of the age you will then be like Him. For you will see Him as He is (I John 3:2-3). Blessed challenge! And better still, blessed prospect!

# Blessed, the Merciful

*"Blessed are the merciful: for they shall obtain mercy."*—Matt. 5:7

At this point it is well to recall our treatment of Matthew 5:3-6. These studies spoke of conviction, repentance, faith, and sanctification. They are the elements in the Christian being "in Christ" (II Cor. 5:17). But as a Christian you are also involved in relations with other people. It is of these relations that Jesus spoke in Matthew 5:7-12.

"Blessed are the merciful: for they shall obtain mercy." One interpreter calls this "a self-acting law of the moral world." What we wish to receive we are to give. And our unwillingness to give it to others may mean that we have not received it from God. Furthermore, even the Christian should not be merciful simply for the purpose of obtaining mercy. Such would be selfishness, not the Christian role of mercy. But it is true that we reap what we sow. By the same token, as a Christian you should be gracious and merciful toward other people (see Matt. 18:23 ff.).

What is the meaning of "mercy"? It translates a Greek word which means *active pity.* It is not a passive but an active word. Its Hebrew equivalent is an even more picturesque word. It means to get inside another person's skin so as to become completely identified with him. In this way you see life through his eyes, think with his mind, feel with his feelings, and react to his experiences as he does. The Hebrew word is stronger but somewhat akin to the Greek word from which comes the English word *sympathy*: to suffer with another.

How does this merciful attitude relate to your Christian life? It lies in the area of *Christian service.* You were saved to serve. As a vessel sanctified to God's use, you are to be actively engaged in serving God through serving others. Lighted by His love and grace, you are to shine in the darkness of the world. Being merciful is letting your light so shine before men that they, seeing your good works, may glorify your heavenly Father.

In the sense of getting into another's skin, mercy depicts understanding and a willingness to forgive. God knows about our struggles with temptation. For this very reason Jesus is our sympathetic high priest (Heb. 4:15). And out of love and grace He forgives us when we confess our sins (I John 1:9). Since He so forgives us, we ought to forgive others.

Mercy is Christian love in action. When John said that "God is love" (I John 4:8) he used the word *agape,* whose basic meaning is absolute loyalty to its object. In this sense you do not have to agree with someone in order to love him. For "God commendeth his love toward us, in that, while we were yet sinners, Christ died for us" (Rom. 5:8). Since He so loved us, we should likewise love one another.

In a sense Jesus touched on this attitude of mercy when He gave the Golden Rule (Matt. 7:12). In effect He said that you should think of something good that you would like someone to do for you; then do that for him. Certainly this includes the merciful attitude toward others in their problems and weaknesses.

It is not always easy to be merciful and forgiving. But by God's grace you can be so. And you may be certain that such an attitude sent forth by you will return in blessings a thousandfold. The greatest will be the knowledge and joy that in some small measure you have emulated the infinite mercy of God toward you.

# Blessed, the Pure in Heart

*"Blessed are the pure in heart: for they shall see God."*—Matt. 5:8

This beatitude should strike a responding note in every Christian's heart. For each of us should desire to achieve this quality.

The Jews of Jesus' day were familiar with ceremonial cleansing. They practiced rituals designed to cleanse the hands and body (Mark 7:1-23), but were not so careful about the inner cleansing of the heart. Jesus reminded His disciples that not what entered the body defiles, but what comes out of the mouth (Matt. 15:11). It is out of the heart that the mouth speaks. So in describing a kingdom citizen the Lord stressed purity of heart as one of his characteristics. "The heart" connotes your inner self—your mind, feelings, and will. If your heart is defiled, then your entire life will be such. Conversely, if your heart is pure, then your life will be likewise.

The word translated "pure" is *katharos,* from which comes the English word *cathartic.* It has to do with cleansing.

Actually the word means "unmixed, unadulterated, without alloy." An example would be pure gold, such is without alloy. As applied to the heart it means a heart with unmixed motives, or one that is loyal under all circumstances. Such a heart is characterized by simplicity or integrity, and is free of duplicity. Such a pure, loyal heart will be concentrated entirely on God and His will.

In this same manner the kingdom citizen should be completely devoted to his King. As such you will serve Him with a pure heart, one which can be trusted. A pure heart is to be compared with the *single eye* as opposed to the evil or sick eye (Matt. 6:22-23). A single eye has perfect vision; an evil eye has a split vision or an astigmatism. One interpreter likened a person with an evil eye to one who is "cock-eyed." If your vision is single, then it is focused on God. If it is evil, then one eye is fastened on God while the other is fixed on the things of this world. Our Lord said that it is impossible for you to be a slave to both God and mammon (the money god; see Matt. 6:24). Each demands absolute loyalty, and you cannot give this to both.

Jesus said that the pure in heart will see God. This figure is drawn from the Oriental court where the king lived in seclusion. The people had access to him only through a trusted official. This official had to be someone who was absolutely loyal to his sovereign. Such a minister could approach the ruler at all times.

It is in this sense that the pure in heart will see God. That person can come into the King's presence because the King knows that his loyalty is unquestioned; the King's will is his will. Such purity of heart can come only through the redemptive work of Christ and the sanctification of the Holy Spirit (Heb. 4:15-16).

Such a ready access to God is suggestive of *communion* and *prayer*. As a child of God you have this wonderful privilege. To know the presence of God in His Holy Spirit and to have access to His throne of grace through His Son is a double, unspeakable blessing.

The author of Hebrews exhorts you by the merit of your Savior to come boldly to the throne of grace and there to find grace to help "in time of need." One version translates this "in the nick of time." There is nothing which you cannot discuss with your heavenly Father. No burden is too heavy to lay at His feet. Even your highest joy will be made infinite as you share it with Him.

For the average citizen to get an audience with the president of the United States would be a most difficult, if not impossible, task. But as a citizen of God's kingdom you have ready access to the King of kings—if you have a pure heart with undivided loyalty to Him. As a son of God you can approach Him without fear or hesitation through your elder Brother, the Son of God.

> When we have exhausted our store of endurance,
> When our strength has failed ere the day is half done,
> When we reach the end of our hoarded resources
> Our Father's full giving is only begun.
>
> His love has no limit. His grace has no measure,
> His power no boundary known unto men;
> For out of His infinite riches in Jesus
> He giveth, and giveth, and giveth again.
>
> Annie Johnson Flint

# Blessed, the Peacemakers

*"Blessed are the peacemakers: for they shall be called the children of God."*—Matt. 5:9

Men the world over are searching for peace: peace between nations, within nations, between men, and within men. But such a quest is futile outside the will of God and the reign of His Son. For Christ is the Prince of Peace (Isa. 9:6). He is the Christian's peace (Eph. 2:13-14). As a Christian you have the peace of God which passes understanding (Phil. 4:7). The world knows no such peace. But to you as a Christian Jesus says, "Peace I leave with you, my peace I give unto you: not as the world giveth, give I unto you. Let not your heart be troubled, neither let it be afraid" (John 14:27).

But as a Christian you are not merely to enjoy this peace, you are to share it. That is why Jesus said, "Blessed are the peacemakers." Christ is the peacemaker between God and man (Col. 1:20-22) and between man and man (Eph. 2:12-18). As a Christian you also are to be a peacemaker. The gospel is the message of peace; so you are to share the gospel with all men. This immediately suggests the *missionary motive.* Or call it evangelism, if you wish. It is the same thing. This is true whether it be bearing your witness for Christ across the ocean or across the street. It may even be a witness borne in your own home.

Since this peace is one of the inner man, it must be brought into each heart. Until men are at peace with God, they cannot be at peace with themselves or with each other.

At Christmastime we sing of "peace on earth, good will toward men" (Luke 2:14, KJV). This sounds like a prophecy concerning peace. But the Greek text reads, "Peace on earth in the sphere of men of good will" or "in men well-pleasing" to God. Thus it is not a prophecy, but a statement of the condition which brings peace among men. It is among men who are well-pleasing to God, or Christian people. So the greatest contribution you and I can make toward peace is to lead men to become well-pleasing to God through faith in His Son. We should lead them to be reconciled to God and then to one another.

One of the greatest statements in this regard is found in Ephesians 1:13-16. This letter was written to several churches in Asia Minor which had both Jews and Gentiles in their fellowship. One of the worst racial problems of all times existed between these two groups. But here they were enjoying Christian fellowship together. Paul says that this was made possible through the redeeming work of Christ. He spoke of the Gentiles or former pagans as having been "far off" but who had been "made nigh by the blood of Christ" (v. 13). "For he is our [Jews' and Gentiles'] peace, who hath made both one, and hath broken down the middle wall of partition between us" (v. 14). This "middle wall" was an allusion to signs which under penalty of death forbade Gentiles to go beyond the Court of the Gentiles in the Jewish temple in Jerusalem. In His death Christ removed these so that Jews and Gentiles alike had direct access to God through Him. Thus He abolished the racial enmity, "for to make in himself of twain one new man, so making peace" (v. 15). This was possible because He had reconciled both Jew and Gentile to God (v. 16).

"To make of twain [two] . . . one new man" suggests an equation of the Christian life. One Jew plus one Gentile plus Christ equals two new men, both Christians. Or one black man plus one white man plus Christ equals two Christian brethren. Any combination of differences—racial, national, social, economic—yields the same result.

The Christian is to be a peacemaker, helping to bring this about through the gospel. While you as one Christian may not be able arbitrarily to produce this result between all men, you should be making the effort within your own sphere of influence. And you should heed the words of Paul in Romans 14:19: "Let us therefore follow after the things which make for peace, and things wherewith one may edify another" (see II Cor. 13:11). And Romans 12:18: "If it be possible, as much as lieth in you, live peaceably with all men." This means that the cause of strife should never originate in you. Your life should send forth the elements and grounds for peace, regardless of what others may do.

Thus you "shall be called the children of God." To be called such means to be such. It is more than relationship; it connotes character. For the name describes the nature. By your efforts at being a peacemaker, others will recognize that you are a child of God.

# Blessed, the Persecuted

*"Blessed are they which are persecuted for righteousness' sake: for theirs is the kingdom of heaven. Blessed are ye, when men shall revile you, and persecute you, and say all manner of evil against you falsely, for my sake. Rejoice, and be exceeding glad: for great is your reward in heaven: for so persecuted they the prophets which were before you."*—Matt. 5:10-12

Here is another paradox. When viewed through unsanctified eyes, persecution appears to be anything but a blessing. But when seen in the light of eternity it is the basis for rejoicing.

All of the qualities involved in verses 3-9 call for the separated life. If your life is separated from the world, you may expect to experience the world's hatred (John 15:18-19). But the Christian should *rejoice* in it, for he is a citizen of the kingdom of heaven. He should not expect to be rewarded for his devotion by the world. The Christian's reward awaits him in heaven.

Of course, there is no basis for joy if one is persecuted for wrongdoing. Peter said that when you suffer it should be not for crimes committed against society but because you are a Christian (I Peter 2:11 ff.; 3:14 ff.).

For the Christian to be blessed or to rejoice in being persecuted, it must come as the result of his loyalty to Christ. It should be for doing right, not wrong. Your life should be such that all persecution is done "falsely" and for the sake of Christ.

Jesus does not ask you to endure what He has not endured. As the unregenerated world hated Him, it will hate you. You are an heir to both His glory and His sufferings (Rom. 8:17). But when you draw up a trial balance of life, you will find that the glory and reward in heaven will outweigh infinitely the sufferings endured on earth.

The Christian's purpose in life is not to please men but to please God (Gal. 1:10). And he is to look to God and not to the world for his reward (I Cor. 4:1-5). Your life as a Christian should be a judgment against the world and its evil. And the world will retaliate in its own way. In our sophisticated age it may or may not be through violence, but in its subtle way it will express its hatred for the Christian. And this expression will demand even greater stability on your part. Inwardly the world appreciates your Christian virtues, but to escape self-condemnation it strikes out at that which it admires.

Of course, you may even be persecuted by those who hold to religious beliefs. The pages of history are crimson stained by the persecution of Christians against other Christians. There is no fanaticism so great as that which is rooted in religious convictions. The Jews thought that they were serving God when they persecuted the Christians. Even Saul of Tarsus did this. But after he became a Christian, Paul's former actions ever pricked his conscience.

The greatest testimony that you can give to your faith as a Christian is displayed in not striking back. When reviled, you should not revile again. This is not easy. But through prayer and devotion to God, you will find grace to do this. As a human being I enjoy being well received by all people. But the only criticism which really bothers me is when I know that it is justified. When criticism is not justified you should ignore it, and go on serving the Lord.

There is a lesson for each of us in an experience of Nehemiah. He and his colleagues had finished rebuilding the walls of Jerusalem. All this had been done in the face of the opposition of hostile neighbors. Though the walls were finished, the gates of the city had not been erected. At this time these hostile neighbors came seeking a conference with Nehemiah. "But," said he, "they thought to do me mischief" (Neh. 6:2). Here was his reply. "I am doing a great work, so that I cannot come down: why should the work cease, whilst I leave it, and come down to you?" (Neh. 6:3).

No Christian should ever stoop to the level of those who persecute him. For he has a great work to do. He cannot do God's work and at the same time live in the jungle of tooth and talon. Rather he should rejoice in his troubles as he goes on serving the Lord.

Men may *revile* you. But God will *reward* you. In His abiding presence through Christ and His Spirit He will give to you blessedness, or the state of sufficiency in living a full, rich life for Him. This blessedness is uncaused or unchanged by outward circumstances. It is entirely the work of God.

# The Greater Blessedness

*"Remember the words of the Lord Jesus, how he said, It is more blessed to give than to receive."*—Acts 20:35

Were it not for Paul this beatitude of Jesus would have been lost. And the loss would be beyond words to describe it.

So often when we think of blessings we think of what we have received. Jesus looked beyond this to the higher blessedness experienced in what we give. Indeed, this brief sentence may well be a summation of His life on earth. He came not to *get* but to *give.* And if we would truly follow Him, this should be the primary purpose of our lives.

Of course, many may be like the man who said that receiving was good enough for him. But will this attitude stand up under close inspection?

Would you rather be a beggar than a benefactor? A patient than a physician? A pauper than a philanthropist? A parasite than a producer? The taught than the teacher?

To give means that you have resources out of which to give. These resources may be either material or spiritual. But to share material possessions means that you have the spiritual quality of generosity. The source of each of these is God. Only as you are in the center of God's will may you find the greater blessedness of giving. "For God so loved...that he gave" (John 3:16).

Man is the crown of God's creative work. And the crown of His redemptive work is a Christian who recognizes that he is a steward of all that he possesses, both material and spiritual. For it is through these dedicated servants that God proposes to share His bounties with others.

Phillips Brooks reminds us that "no grace or blessing is truly ours until God has blessed some one else with it through us." The world recognizes with its honor the philanthropist and his large gifts. But even though most of us cannot make such gifts, God honors us for the sharing of what we have. It may be a coin, a word of cheer, a witness borne for Christ. But none of them goes without the pleasing smile of Him who gives bountifully to all.

Jean Paul Richter said, "Do not wait for extraordinary circumstances to do good actions; try to use ordinary situations."

> The best portion of a good man's life—
> His little, nameless, unremembered acts
>   Of kindness and love.
>
> William Wordsworth

Charles Haddon Spurgeon was one of the greatest preachers in history. One of the most profound things he ever said about living the Christian life is stated in simple terms in two sentences: "Be good; get good; and do good. Do all the good you can, to all the people you can, in all the ways you can, as often as ever you can, as long as you can."

If you will follow this simple program in life, you will realize the greater blessedness. For you will experience that truly "it is more blessed to give than to receive."

There is a divinity that shapes our ends,
Rough-hew them how we will.
William Shakespeare

# AMID LIFE'S CERTAINTIES

# The Bible

*"The grass withereth, and the flower thereof falleth away: but the word of the Lord endureth for ever."*—I Peter 1:24-25

So obvious is this blessing that many people ignore it. Chaucer's words sadly apply to many who profess to believe the Bible. "His studie was but lited on the bible." Which poses a question for each one of us. Someone asked, "If God is a reality and the soul is a reality, and you are an immortal being, what are you doing with your Bible shut?" In this light let us note what others have said about the Bible.

The Bible is the inspired Word of God. Literally, the Bible is "God-breathed" (II Tim. 3:16; II Peter 1:21). It is God's written Word revealing Christ, the living Word. For He is the final criterion by which the Bible is to be interpreted. This is why, in the words of Samuel Taylor Coleridge, "it finds me at a greater depth of my being than any other book." President Woodrow Wilson said, "When you have read the Bible you will know it is the Word of God because you will have found it the key to your own heart, your own happiness, and your own duty." John Locke said, "The Bible is one of the greatest blessings bestowed by God on the children of men. It has God for its author, salvation for its end, and truth without any mixture of error for its matter. It is all pure, all sincere; nothing too much; nothing wanting."

In the Middle Ages, when the Bible was practically unavailable to the common man, we are told that a peasant would pay the price of a wagonload of hay for the privilege of reading it for fifteen minutes—while it was chained to a column in a church.

It is difficult to understand why you and I do not read the Bible more. Is it because familiarity with its presence in the home has bred contempt for it? If your Bible is just a decoration in the home, then for you its message cannot avail. But if read—and studied—it is veritably God's Word for your hungry soul. And as H. C. Trumbull says, "A loving trust in the Author of the Bible is the best preparation for a wise and profitable study of the Bible itself."

A knowledge and practice of the Bible's truths can give stability and strength to your spiritual life. "Thy word have I hid in mine heart, that I might not sin against thee" (Ps. 119:11). As your body must be nourished by food, so your spirit must feed on God's Word. It is not only a lamp unto your feet and a light unto your path, it is bread and meat for your soul.

Furthermore, the reading of the Bible on the part of a people is the best defense against a corrupt social order. Of course, for this to be true, what you read must be the basis of what you do. Thomas Carlyle referred to the Bible as "the book wherein, for thousands of years, the spirit of man has found light and nourishment, and the response to whatever was deepest in his heart."

Daniel Webster may well have been speaking to our generation when he said, "If truth be not diffused, error will be; if God and His Word are not known and received, the devil and his works will gain the ascendancy; if the evangelical volume does not reach every hamlet, the pages of a corrupt and licentious literature will; if the power of the gospel is not felt through the length and breadth of the land, anarchy and misrule, degradation and misery, corruption and darkness, will reign without mitigation or end."

The Bible speaks to the high and lowly, to the saint and sinner alike—and in all circumstances of life. Henry Van Dyke reminds us that "it comes to the palace to tell the monarch that he is a servant to the Most High, and into the cottage to assure the peasant that he is a son of God. Children listen to its stories with wonder and delight, and wise men ponder them as parables of life. It has a word of peace for the time of peril, a word of comfort for the day of calamity, a word of light for the hour of darkness. . . . The wicked and the proud tremble at its warning, but to the wounded and penitent it has a mother's voice. The wilderness and the solitary place have been made glad by it, and the fire on the hearth has lit the reading of its well-worn page. It has woven itself into our deepest affections and colored our dearest dreams so that love and friendship, sympathy and devotion, memory and hope, put on the beautiful garments of its treasured speech, breathing frankincense and myrrh."

Again, the message of the Bible is undergirding strength for a nation. Again quoting Daniel Webster, "If we abide by the principles taught in the Bible, our country will go on prospering and to prosper, but if we and our posterity neglect its instruction and authority, no man can tell how sudden a catastrophe may overwhelm us and bury our glory in profound obscurity."

Thus these sages of yesteryear call us to remember the blessing of the Bible. Like the prophets of old they challenge our hearts and minds to enshrine the Bible in our lives, homes, and institutions. For only thus may it truly be the blessing which God intended it to be.

You may not be in position to challenge all men to obey this truth, but you can see that you and those about you do so. John Ruskin gives to each of us a formula for rich, effective living. Speaking of the Bible he said, "Make it the first morning business of your life to understand some part of the Bible clearly, and make it your daily business to obey it in all that you do understand."

> Holy Bible, Book divine
> Precious treasure, thou art mine:
> Mine to tell me whence I came;
> Mine to teach me what I am. . . .
>
> Mine to tell of joys to come,
> And the rebel sinner's doom:
> O thou holy Book divine,
> Precious treasure, thou art mine.
>
> John Burton, Sr.

# Our Heavenly Father

*"Our Father which art in heaven."*—Matt. 6:9

Doubtless you have heard the story about the prayer of the little girl during the London air raids of World War II. Having finished her prayer about many things she closed with words something like these: "And, dear God, please take care of yourself. For if anything happened to you, I don't know what we would do."

Perhaps we may smile at this child's simple theology. But when things go wrong do not many people wonder if something has happened to God? Is He dead? Has He run away, leaving us in the lurch? Is He indifferent to our needs? Or powerless to act? Or, worse still, does He have the power but doesn't care?

In such moments of questionings it is most heartening to read Psalm 2. Though the heathen may rage and the kings of earth take counsel against God, "He that sitteth in the heavens shall laugh: the Lord shall have them in derision" (v. 4). Like Paul on a stormy sea we can say, "Wherefore, sirs, be of good cheer [courage]: for I believe God" (Acts 27:25).

The Bible teaches that God is eternal, all-wise, all-powerful, and present in every moment of time and space. He is the universe but not contained by it; He is the creator of the universe and the director of history, guiding it toward His benevolent purpose. He is holiness, righteousness, truth, and love. And His love characterizes His being and actions in every one of His other attributes.

However, while the Old Testament primarily presents God as high and lifted up, it was Jesus who taught that He is our heavenly Father. He embodies in perfection all of the noble attributes of fatherhood. This does not teach the universal Fatherhood of God. But it does mean that God is fatherly in His nature, and longs to be the heavenly Father of all men. He is Father in truth only to those who have become His children through faith in His Son (John 1:12).

As your heavenly Father, God is infinite love (I John 4:8). His is a holy and righteous love. For this reason He cannot condone sin. He loves the sinner, but hates his sin. He hates sin for what it is—rebellion against His benevolent will—and for what it does to you. He wills only good for you; sin works only bad for you. As a Father He chastises His children (Heb. 12:6-11). but is bountiful in forgiveness for all who repent and confess their sins (I John 1:9). William Cowper reminds you that

> Behind a frowning Providence
> He hides a shining face.

Your heavenly Father is gracious. He saves you by grace, keeps you by grace, and by grace enables you to be His obedient and loving child.

As your heavenly Father, God loves to give good gifts to you (Matt. 7:11; Luke 11:10-13). He is the giver of every good and perfect gift (James 1:17). But as a Father He longs for your thanksgiving and the proper use of His gifts. He permits you to enter into trials or testings. But He does not tempt you to do evil (James 1:13). He will not let you be tested beyond endurance, but gives you strength to overcome (I Cor. 10:13). His word to you is ever to "submit yourselves therefore to God. Resist the devil, and he will flee from you. Draw nigh to God, and he will draw nigh to you" (James 4:7-8).

As a Christian you are a child of God. You are an heir of God and a joint-heir with God's eternal Son (Rom. 8:17). You are a joint-heir to both glory and suffering. But in the end the glory far outweighs the suffering. And as Paul says to the Corinthians, "I am filled with comfort, I am exceeding joyful in all our tribulation" (II Cor. 7:4).

It is quite evident that as our Father, God does not exempt us from the problems and troubles which are common to all men. He is not seeking hothouse plants, but giant oaks that have withstood the storms of the elements. Neither does He seal us in plastic bags which separate us from the world's ills. Rather He desires that we will be salt and light to a world which decays in darkness. But whatever the trial which at times may seem to overwhelm us, we can rest secure in the knowledge that not even a sparrow falls without His notice and concern. Surely then He cares for us.

Because God is your Father you need have no fear as to what men may do to you. Since God is righteous love, you know that in the end truth will prevail. In the meantime, in thoughts expressed by James Russell Lowell, you can know that while truth may seem forever to be on the scaffold and wrong upon the throne, that scaffold sways the future. And beyond the dim unknown God stands in the shadows, keeping watch over His own.

# Our Elder Brother

*"For both he that sanctifieth and they that are sanctified are all one: For which cause he is not ashamed to call them brethren."*—Heb. 2:11

"Thanks be unto God for his unspeakable gift" (II Cor. 9:15)! Thus in tones which defy expression Paul spoke of the gift of God's love, His Son Jesus Christ. The exact word rendered "unspeakable" is not found anywhere in Scripture prior to this instance. A kindred word found in a non-Biblical writing means "wonder beyond description." So when the apostle could find no word to describe God's Gift, he coined one to embody his thought. But thanks to him we have this "wonder beyond description" word to describe this blessing that is beyond human language to express it.

The author of Hebrews brings this thought closer in our human experience as he tells how through His death Jesus Christ sanctified us or set us apart as vessels fit for God's service. And in this sanctification we are one with Him. Literally, we are "out of one," out of God. Jesus is God's

Son eternally, and those who believe in Him are the "many sons" mentioned in Hebrews 2:10. In this sense He is *our elder Brother.* For this reason He is not ashamed to call us brothers, even though we may be unworthy sons of God.

This thought about Jesus Christ being our elder Brother is all the more amazing when we remember that He is the eternal God who as the Son reveals God as redeeming love. In so doing He became "flesh, and dwelt among us, (and we beheld his glory, the glory as of the only begotten of the Father,) full of grace and truth . . . and of his fulness have all we received, and grace for grace" (John 1:14, 16).

Jesus Christ was and is God. But even more glorious is the truth that God *became* Jesus of Nazareth. Thus Jesus is the God-Man. It is just as great an error to deny His humanity as to deny His deity, for both were present in Him in a manner beyond our comprehension. Conceived by the Holy Spirit in the virgin Mary's womb, He was God's Son. But He was Mary's son also. He was perfect in both deity and humanity. And as the Son of Man He is the perfect humanity which God wills that all men shall be.

Jesus identified Himself with humanity completely, apart from sin. He subjected Himself to the limitations of flesh: He entered history as a baby, grew into manhood, learned to walk and talk as other children; He worked by the sweat of His brow even as you and I do. Yet His wisdom infinitely exceeded that of any other man. He knew hunger, thirst, and weariness. He was tempted as man, yet without sin (Heb. 4:15). He proved that God was just in His righteous demands on men; for, even though He lived in a corrupt world, He did not commit sin. Then He showed God as the justifier (Rom. 3:26) as in His death He was made sin for us that through faith in Him we might receive God's righteousness as a gift of His grace (II Cor. 5:21). Though men slew Him God raised Him from the dead, and He is seated at God's right hand waiting until His enemies become His footstool (Heb. 10:12-13). He is coming again to receive His own unto Himself (Heb. 9:28). And He lives ever to hold intercession before God for us (I John 2:1). He is truly "Emmanuel... God with us" (Matt. 1:23)!

Martin Luther summarized what Christ means to you and me. "In his life Christ is an example showing us how to live; in his death, he is a sacrifice satisfying for our sins; in his resurrection, a conqueror; in his ascension, a king; in his intercession, a high priest." Ralph Waldo Emerson said, "The name of Jesus is not so much written as plowed into the history of the world." The historian Ernest Renan said that "all history is incomprehensible without Christ." Phillips Brooks exclaimed, "Jesus Christ, the condescension of deity and the exaltation of humanity."

All of this causes us to stand before Him in wonder, love, and praise. Scarcely less wonderful than the incarnation itself is the fact that one so infinitely great is not ashamed to call us His brothers. Partaking of the nature of both God and man, in His person both meet in reconciliation. And for this reason God is our Father, Christ is our Brother, and we can in Him come boldly to God's throne of grace (Heb. 4:16).

So as you count your blessings, do not forget to thank God for His "unspeakable gift." Though He ascended to the Father, He is still with us "alway, even unto the end of the world [age]" (Matt. 28:20). "Alway," literally should read, "all the days." Days of joy and sorrow, days of triumph and defeat—all the days. As one said, "The ascension has not taken Him away from you, but it has carried you up to Him." He has gone to prepare a place for you, that where He is, you may be also (John 14:3). And He is coming again to receive His own.

For the Christian, this life is but a rehearsal for all who will eternally sing "a new song, saying, Thou art worthy to take the book, and to open the seals thereof: for thou wast slain, and hast redeemed us to God by thy blood out of every kindred, and tongue, and people, and nation; and hast made us unto our God kings and priests: and we shall reign on the earth.... Worthy is the Lamb that was slain to receive power, and riches, and wisdom, and strength, and honour, and glory, and blessing" (Rev. 5:9, 10, 12).

It is a thought which defies our understanding. But, thanks be to God, He who is our Lord and Savior is also our Brother! Such a relationship entails an equal responsibility to share its glorious privilege with all men everywhere.

> The world's great heart is aching,
>   Aching fiercely in the night;
> And God alone can heal it,
>   And God alone give light;
> And the ones to take that message—
>   To bear the living Word—
> Are you and I, my Brothers,
>   And the millions who have heard.

# Our Divine Helper

*"And I will pray the Father, and he shall give you another Comforter, that he may abide with you for ever."*—John 14:16

This wonderful promise was made by Jesus to His disciples the night before His death. For three and one-half years they had known the glory of His bodily presence. Soon they would be left behind as He returned to His Father. To His followers this meant that they would be alone in the world. To dispel their fears Jesus said, "I will not leave you comfortless: I will come to you" (John 14:18). "Comfortless" translates a Greek word from which comes our word *orphan*. They would not be left as orphans. He would come to them in the presence and power of His Holy Spirit (v. 17).

Jesus called the Holy Spirit "another Comforter." The word rendered "another" means "another of the same kind." So He will be another of the same kind as Jesus had been. "Comforter" translates a word which is anglicized as *Paraclete*. It means "one who is called alongside." Of Jesus in I

John 2:1 it is rendered as "advocate." This word comes from the Latin *ad voco,* meaning "to call to." The Greek word was used of a lawyer, especially one for the defense. In this sense Jesus is our advocate before the Father; and the Holy Spirit is God's advocate before the tribunal of men's hearts as He convicts the lost of sin, righteousness, and judgment (John 16:8-11).

However, with respect to the Christian this word may also read "exhorter," "encourager," or "consoler." This is why I have chosen to use the more inclusive term "divine helper." The Holy Spirit is in the world to be our helper both in our personal needs and in our efforts to work for the Lord.

Note that Jesus said that He would pray the Father and the Father would give this divine helper. This does not mean that He had not been in the world from the beginning. At times He is called the Spirit of God; at other times He is called the Spirit of Christ. In essence, the meaning is the same. He is the Spirit of God sent forth to do His work. This is seen in the Old Testament. But it is more evident in the New Testament. What Jesus meant in His promise was that the Holy Spirit would come in power to carry on the work which He had begun.

Do you find it easier to understand Jesus than the Holy Spirit? This is as it should be. For in the Christian era the Spirit's role is to testify to and glorify Jesus, not Himself (John 16:13-15). As "another of the same kind of Comforter" the Holy Spirit is Jesus' other self or, as one has called Him, "the Other Jesus." It is in Him that Jesus is with you "alway, even unto the end of the world [age]" (Matt. 28:20).

Doubtless each of us at one time or other has wished that he could have been in Palestine with Jesus when He was on earth. However, we have an even greater privilege; for when Jesus was on earth He dwelt *among* men; but now the Holy Spirit dwells *in* the Christian (John 14:17; I Cor. 6:19). At times the disciples were away from Jesus' presence; you are never away from the Spirit's presence. Jesus worked with, spoke to, and motivated men from without; the Holy Spirit does this from within you. At most Jesus was with His disciples only about three and one-half years. The Holy Spirit abides forever. He came in power at Pentecost for His special dispensation. And He has never been taken out of the world. When you became a Christian the Holy Spirit took up His abode in you (John 14:17; Acts 10:44-45). He sealed you as God's purchased possession. And His presence is God's guarantee that you are saved and secured as His own (Eph. 1:13-14). Thus you are filled with the Holy Spirit. But you can be filled with His power only as you yield yourself to Him and His work. It is not a question as to how much of the Spirit you have, but how much of you He has. Since your body is the temple of the Holy Spirit you should not defile it but use it for God's glory (I Cor. 6:19-20).

Some people associate the Spirit's presence with ecstatic experiences. It should be remembered, however, that the phenomena of the sound of wind and flames like tongues of fire at Pentecost were passing phenomena. According to I Corinthians 13:8 "tongues... shall cease." But the abiding element of Pentecost is the Holy Spirit's presence and power to enable you to do the Lord's work.

Paul does not list the ecstatic experiences as "fruit of the Spirit." Rather he lists this fruit as "love, joy, peace, long-suffering, gentleness, goodness, faith, meekness, temperance" or self-control (Gal. 5:22-23).

We are not told to seek the ecstatic experiences. But every Christian should seek to bear in his life the "fruit of the Spirit." Thus you will be blessed, and will be a blessing.

# The Greatest Love

*"For God so loved the world, that he gave his only begotten Son, that whosoever believeth in him should not perish, but have everlasting life."*—John 3:16

If the love of our fellow beings is precious to us, how much more so is the love of God! First John 4:8 tells us that "God is love." It is His nature to love. He can no more cease to love than He can cease to be God. Basically the Greek word used for God's love means absolutely loyalty to its object.

God's love is a holy, righteous love. Therefore, while He loves you, He hates your sin. He hates sin for what it does to both Himself and to you.

God loves us not because of what we are, but in spite of what we are. It is one thing to love one's friends. But it takes a greater love to love one's enemies. "But God commendeth his love toward us, in that, while we were yet sinners, Christ died for us" (Rom. 5:8). Thus it is that God loves us even when we live in rebellion against His benevolent will.

Love reveals itself. And God's greatest revelation of His

love is in His only begotten Son who died to save us from our sin. This is the gospel, the glad tidings of salvation which God offers to all men who will believe in His Son.

John 3:16 is perhaps the best-known and best-loved verse in the Bible. It is the gospel within the gospel. If all of the Bible except this one verse was lost, there is enough gospel in it to save the entire human race.

It speaks of the greatest Lover. "God." It expresses the greatest degree of love. "So loved." It tells of the greatest object of this love. "The world." It contains the greatest purpose of love. "That." It involves the greatest act of love. "Gave." It declares the greatest gift of love. "His only begotten Son." It connotes the universal nature of God's love. "Whosoever." It tells of the greatest response to His love. "Believeth on him." It declares the greatest deliverance of love. "Should not perish." It involves the greatest alternative of love. "But." It proclaims the greatest result of God's love. "Have everlasting life."

It is no wonder then that God's love is the infinite love. It characterizes and governs every attribute of His nature. Even His chastisement is given in love that He might bring men to repentance and faith, and, thereafter, develop them into His fruitful servants.

God's love wills the greatest good for the greatest number of people. It is because sin hinders this benevolent will that God hates it. And He has done all that even God can do to destroy its evil power in your life.

This is why unbelief toward Christ is the greatest of sins. For it spurns God's love and redemptive work. It treads under profane feet the very blood of the Son of God given for your redemption.

God loves you too much to save you against your will. For

such would destroy your personality and turn you into a puppet. In His wise benevolence He has made you a person endowed with the right of choice. You are free to choose. But freedom entails responsibility. So you are responsible for your choices.

In love God has taken the initiative in salvation. But for it to be effective in your life, you must respond to it in repentance toward God and faith in His Son.

What Sir Walter Scott said of the love which God has deposited in the human breast is infinitely true when spoken of God's love for man.

> True Love's the gift which God has given
> To man alone beneath the heaven:
> It is not fantasy's hot fire,
>   Whose wishes soon as granted fly;
> It liveth not in fierce desire,
>   With dead desire it doth not die;
> It is the secret sympathy,
>   The silver link, the silken tie,
> Which heart to heart and mind to mind
>   In body and in soul doth bind.

# God's Providence

*"He maketh his sun to rise on the evil and on the good, and sendeth rain on the just and on the unjust."*—Matt. 5:45

We often hear it said that the good suffer with the bad. That is true. But equally true is the fact that in certain ways God blesses the evil along with the good. This does not mean that He is morally and spiritually indifferent. It means that God is love, and for that reason He bestows His natural blessings without respect to persons.

God's work with men may be seen in creation, providence, and redemption. He created all men, provides for their needs, and has provided redemption for all who will receive it through faith in His Son.

This present thought centers on God's providence. *Providence* may be read as *provide*-ence. God provides. What man does with it is another matter.

Given fertile soil, the two ingredients necessary for a good harvest are sun and rain. And God provides them for all men regardless of their personal relation to Him. The sun does not inquire as to a farmer's spiritual condition before shining on his land. Neither does a cloud do so before dropping its rain. The sun shines; the rain falls. And both good and bad are blessed thereby.

However, once God has given these blessings, men play a vital part in the final result. The same soil, sun, and rain will grow weeds as well as corn or tomatoes. So if a farmer is to receive the intended benefits from God's providence he must use them properly. God gives the ingredients, but man must plant the seed and till the soil if he is to have the desired harvest.

Hebrews 6:7-8 expresses this idea. "For the earth which drinketh in the rain that cometh oft upon it, and bringeth forth herbs meet for them by whom it is dressed, receiveth blessing from God: but that which beareth thorns and briers is rejected, and is nigh unto cursing; whose end is to be burned."

Farmers gather fruits and grain into storage places. They pile up thorns and briers and burn them. God gathers His own unto Himself. But that which is the fruit of evil, He commits to fire (Gen. 3:17-18).

So the providence of God looks beyond the material to the spiritual. Christians should use God's blessings to serve Him. Sadly, many abuse them, not to the loss of their souls, but to the loss of a life which should be used for God (I Cor. 3:11-15).

What about the unsaved person? Paul says that God's purpose in giving him natural blessings is to the end that they may enable God to give that person the greatest blessing. For, said Paul, "The goodness of God leadeth thee to repentance" (Rom. 2:4). That is, God intends that you will so respond to

His benevolence. As you read these words, will you search your heart as to your relationship to God in Christ? And having received Him as your Savior through repentance and faith, will you determine to use God's blessings for His glory? In this way you will be infinitely blessed indeed.

# Peace

*"Thou wilt keep him in perfect peace, whose mind is stayed on thee: because he trusteth in thee."*—Isa. 26:3

If I should ask you what it is that you desire in life more than anything else, what would you answer? For most of us it could be expressed in one word: peace. The ancient Jews greeted each other with that word: shalom.

The ideal of history is a society in which nations will live in perfect peace (Isa. 65:17-25). But the Bible teaches that this will not be realized until Christ reigns supreme. In history as we know it, Jesus said that "wars and rumours of wars" will continue to the end of the age (Matt. 24:6). These things do not themselves herald the end of the age, but due to evil in men's hearts they are a part of history itself.

The historians Will and Ariel Durant tell us that "in the last 3,421 years of recorded history only 268 have seen no war."[1] And though we may strive for "peace for the next

---

1. *The Lessons of History* (New York: Simon and Schuster, 1968), p. 81.

century," such is not likely to be achieved so long as Satan has a hand in men's affairs.

But the wonderful promises of peace may be realized in the heart of every believer in the Lord Jesus Christ. For God's peace is not contingent on circumstances which surround us. It is the quietude that God can give in the midst of a storm. It was of this peace that Jesus spoke when He said, "Peace I leave with you, my peace I give unto you: not as the world giveth, give I unto you. Let not your heart be troubled, neither let it be afraid" (John 14:27).

When our Lord spoke these words the dark clouds of Calvary loomed before Him. His little band of disciples would be caught in the teeth of a tempest unlike any other that the world has seen. And for the rest of their lives they would know stormy times as they sought to evangelize the world.

Yet Jesus spoke of *peace*. It was not the world's peace, which is given and taken away. It was His abiding peace, no matter what the future might hold. What the world calls peace may be stagnation. But the peace of God which defies human comprehension is serenity of soul as the world's storms rage.

Someone wisely said, "Peace doth not dwell in outward things, but within the soul; we may preserve it in the midst of the bitterest pain, if our will remains firm and submissive. Peace in this life springs from acquiescence, not in an exemption from suffering."

The richest depth of peace comes not only in trusting in God your Savior. It is also enhanced as in that faith you do your duty as He has laid it out before you. If John 14 speaks of peace, John 15 speaks of duty. It is fruitbearing as you abide in Christ and His will. He suffered in doing His Father's will. You can expect to do no less. But He has promised the Holy Spirit, our divine helper, who will enable us to rise above the current scene as we do the will of our redeeming God.

> Peace does not mean the end of our striving;
> Joy does not mean the drying of our tears;
> Peace is the power that comes to souls arriving
> Up to the light where God Himself appears.
> G. A. Studdert-Kennedy

Because of God's peace which abides within, you can go about your daily duties serene and secure. To each believer, therefore, Victor Hugo spoke when he said, "When you have accomplished your daily task, go sleep in peace; God is awake."

# Chastisement

*"For whom the Lord loveth he chasteneth, and scourgeth every son whom he receiveth."*—Heb. 12:6

Chastisement may seem to be in strange company when it is listed among our blessings. But when rightly understood, the strangeness disappears. The Greek verb rendered "chasteneth" means to train as a child. "Scourgeth" means to whip. Everyone of us can recall receiving such from our parents (Heb. 12:9-10). A parent chastens his own children, not those of another. And the fact that you endure such from God is evidence that you are His child (Heb. 12:7-8). God disciplines in love, as, indeed, every parent should.

Did you ever suffer for some sin you committed, yet see some godless person do the same with no evident retribution? Perhaps you wonder why this difference. The difference is that you are God's child and the other is not. Do not for one moment think that the godless one escapes punishment. He is but storing up God's wrath against the day of judgment (II Peter 3:7). But God punishes His children within the context of history. And God's *training as a child* is for our good (Heb. 12:11).

This is a difficult lesson for us to learn. But when seen in the light of the whole, it is evident that God chastens us in love and for our benefit. Someone said that

> Heaven is not always angry when He strikes
> But most chastises those whom most He likes.

Thus God should not be regarded as a cosmic policeman or as a sniper aiming His rifle of retribution on those who incur His displeasure. Rather He is a loving Father who disciplines His children that they may be brought up in such a way as to be blessed by doing His benevolent will. His laws are for our good. When we live by them we are blessed. When we live contrary to them, they bring their own punishment. These effects are true whether they are with respect to God's natural, physical, moral, or spiritual laws.

Shakespeare said, "Better a little chiding than a great deal of heartbreak." So God chides His children that they may be brought back into His righteous and benevolent paths. If you accept this chiding and respond to its aim, it will become a blessing to you and to others.

One of David's greatest psalms (Ps. 51) was written to describe his feelings of repentance after the prophet Nathan had revealed to him the terrible nature of his sin with Bathsheba. It should be read, followed by Psalm 32 in which David expressed the blessedness of knowing that his sin had been forgiven. Note that in Psalm 51 he said that if God would forgive him, "Then will I teach transgressors thy ways; and sinners shall be converted unto thee" (v. 13).

> Aromatic plants bestow
> No spicy fragrance while they grow;
> But crushed or trodden to the ground
> Diffuse their sweetness all around.

Oliver Goldsmith

An anonymous writer said that "there is frequently more love in a frown than there could be in a smile." If God smiled on us in our sins, it would be an unwise Providence which would encourage our evil to our undoing. His frown is designed to bring us to our senses that we may live to our blessing and His glory.

I am indebted to T. A. Vassar for the following beautiful illustration of the place of God's chastisement of His children.

> Organs mean melody and beauty, but organ factories mean din and dirt. The instrument is built for music, and music it will ultimately bring, but the building where it is fashioned resounds with more racket than rhythm. The world is such a factory. In it the Master Builder is creating and completing new men in Christ Jesus; making them mete for the inheritance of the saints in light. The process, however, by which the author and finisher of our faith prosecutes and perfects his plans will often be misunderstood. Many of the operations will appear hard and rough, and will hit as heavily and hurt as badly as the raps of the hammer in the shop.[1]

So just remember that when God's chastening rod falls on

---

1. Virginia Ely, *I Quote* (New York: Steward, 1947), p. 47.

you, He designs for you a service which sin would defeat. And if you respond to His loving teaching as one of His children, your repentance and prayer for forgiveness will not only make beautiful music among men. It will rise to heaven's portals as a beautiful symphony making glad the heart of God.

# Health Is...

*"Beloved, I wish above all things that thou mayest prosper and be in health, even as thy soul prospereth."*—III John 2

For years it has been a custom of mine that when I sign an autograph I put beneath it "III John 2." For to me this verse is the best wish that I can make for anyone. It strikes a balance between natural and spiritual health and prosperity. Without the spiritual the natural may prove to be other than a blessing.

Leigh Hunt wrote that "the groundwork of all happiness is health." With this I agree, provided that "health" involves both body and spirit. It is true that sometimes the healthiest soul is housed in an unhealthy body. But a healthy body with a healthy spirit is the ideal. It was perfectly realized in the life of Jesus. And while in this life we will not ever be His equal, He is our goal and guide. So as we look at Jesus we see what true health is.

Health is—*a sound body*. As we humans gauge health, we begin here. This is echoed in the words of Thomas Carlyle:

"There is no kind of achievement equal to perfect health." And yet, most of us take our healthy bodies for granted. We never pause to thank God for a strong constitution or for bodies free from pain.

Furthermore, we abuse our strong bodies. We drive ourselves to distraction in pursuit of life's goals, whether they are fame, power, wealth, or any other achievement we have set for ourselves.

Julia Ward Howe once wrote, "Nature demands that man be ever at the top of his condition. He who violates her laws must pay the penalty though he sit upon a throne. Many a man pays for his success with a slice of his constitution."

The greatest killer today in our nation is that group of diseases related to the heart and circulatory system. A century ago such diseases were scarcely known in America. The prevalence of such today may be explained, at least in part, by the diet we eat, lack of physical exercise, and the stressful pace we maintain. And the sad thing is that, like a dry well, we never miss the blessing of health until through abuse we have lost it.

Someone said, "To insure good health: eat lightly, breathe deeply; live moderately, cultivate cheerfulness, and maintain an interest in life."

Health is—*a sound mind.* And a sound mind involves more than sanity. It encompasses the whole of your attitudes toward life. For instance, optimism is not all physical. But it does contribute to the joy of living. And there is a direct relationship between optimism and a sound body. At the same time pessimism is often a companion to low physical vitality.

Knowing this relationship, Jesus counseled that we should

not be overly anxious about the material and physical aspects of life (Matt. 6:25-34). A divided mind will not extend life, but it may shorten it. In Matthew 6:22-23 Jesus spoke of "single" and "evil" or double, diseased eyes. The person with a single eye is one who fixes his gaze on the true, spiritual values of life. But one with an evil eye is plagued with double vision. One interpreter called him "cock-eyed." He piously rolls one eye heavenward, but the other is focused on the things of earth. It is such a person who is a candidate for ulcers or worse.

This is why Jesus said that you cannot be a slave to both God and mammon (the money god; see Matt. 6:24). Both demand absolute allegiance, and this cannot be given to two different masters. It is also why Jesus counseled you to seek first the kingdom of God and His (or its) righteousness. In other words, your life's purpose should be to witness to others about God's kingdom and its righteousness. Doing so, you should trust Him to provide for life's necessities. And Jesus promised that "all these things shall be added unto you" (Matt. 6:33). As one man said, his business in life was to serve God; he pegged shoes to pay expenses.

Health is—*a sound soul.* This means, first of all, that you have trusted in Jesus Christ as your Savior. Furthermore, it means that you have fitted your will in the center of God's will. Jesus said that He delighted always to do His Father's will (John 4:34, 5:30). And Paul exhorted his readers to be so transformed as to know and do the good and perfect will of God (Rom. 12:1-2).

Writing to his friends in Philippi the apostle said, "Let your moderation [gentleness, sweet reasonableness] be known unto all men.... Be careful [overly anxious] for nothing; but in every thing by prayer and supplication with thanksgiving let your requests be made known unto God. And the peace of God, which passeth all understanding, shall keep [guard] your hearts and minds in Christ Jesus" (Phil. 4:5-7).

# A Godly Home

*"As for me and my house, we will serve the Lord."*—Josh. 24:15

These words are a part of Joshua's farewell address to Israel. Having led the Israelites through the conquest of Canaan, he laid down principles which would enable them to live there in peace and prosperity. He challenged them to settle the issue as to their religious allegiance. No doubt he hoped that they would serve and worship Jehovah, still he knew the choice was theirs to make. God does not force Himself on you. But He longs that your home and life will be built on Him. Joshua made this choice. History reveals that to the degree that the nation did not do this, the nation and its people suffered.

The heart of a nation is its homes. And no nation will be godly if its homes are otherwise. Someone said that "the strength of a nation, especially of a republican nation, is in the intelligent and well-ordered homes of the people."

In years past multitudes of homes had a prayer hanging on

the wall. It read, "God Bless Our Home." One cannot help but feel that the scarcity of these mottoes today is one symptom of the lack of stability of many present-day homes. Horace Bushnell once said, "A house without a roof would scarcely be a more different home than a family unsheltered by God's friendship and the sense of being always rested in His providential care and guidance."

If you are to have a godly home, then you must make it so. By deliberate choice you must determine that you and your house will serve the Lord. This does not mean that the life of the home will be just one continuous prayer meeting or revival meeting. But it does mean that in the family circle the Bible will be read, prayer will be experienced, and the principles of God's righteous will will be ingrained in the character and conduct of the family. Such a home will be a light in the world's darkness. Its members will become leaven of Godlikeness to permeate the social order.

A home that is not genuinely Christian is not a true home. It may be a house, a shelter from the elements, and a gathering place for the family members. But for it to be a home in the truest sense of the word, God must be its center and foundation. Christ must be in the hearts of those who dwell there. And the Holy Spirit must sanctify the home by His unseen but vital presence.

Such a home will be a citadel of righteousness for both church and state. It will give strength to the social order. And it will be a little bit of heaven on earth.

Henry Van Dyke reminds us of the blessings of a godly home.

> The Crown of the Home is Godliness;
> The Beauty of the Home is Order;

The Glory of the Home is Hospitality;
The Blessing of the Home is Contentment.

And where these things abide you can truly sing, "There's no place like home."

Along the cool sequester'd vale of life
They kept the noiseless tenor of their way.

> Thomas Gray

# LIFE'S "COOL SEQUESTER'D" WAY

# On Being a Blessing

*"I will bless thee ... and thou shalt be a blessing."*—Gen. 12:2

Did it ever occur to you that a blessing may become a curse? It may, unless it is properly regarded and used. It can produce a selfishness that only looks for more blessings to be selfishly enjoyed. For this reason the Lord intends that blessings should be shared.

This was the point of God's word to Abraham. He promised to bless him in order that he could be a blessing to others. History records that Abraham's descendants came to think only in terms of being blessed, with little or no thought about being a blessing. This attitude became the undoing of the people of Israel and has been the undoing of many people since. The figure as to what made the Dead Sea dead may be trite, but it is everlastingly true. It is always taking in but never giving out. It receives, but does not give.

We are in the world to serve, not simply to receive. Blessings from God place on us the responsibility to be a blessing to others. Jesus taught that greatness in the kingdom of heaven is gauged not by what we get but by what we give. The world gauges greatness by how many people serve us. God measures greatness by how many we serve. Jesus' example of true service was to serve little children. Beyond the truth of investing our lives in a little child is the greater truth of serving with no thought of reward.

You might serve a man with the selfish motive that he in turn might reward you. But to serve a little child is to serve for service's sake, with no regard as to what the child may do for you.

On one occasion Jesus said that when you give a dinner you should not invite the rich and affluent. Such might be done with the expectation that, in turn, you may be invited to their dinners. Rather Jesus said to invite the poor, lame, and blind, those from whom you do not expect to receive in return.

In Matthew 25 Jesus gave the parable of the judgment. Men were judged on the basis of what they had or had not done for those in need. For, said He, in so doing they had or had not done these things for Him. You are not saved or lost on such a basis, but your actions toward others reveal your relation to Christ. God *graced* us in saving us; we should *grace* others in His name and for His glory. In serving men you are serving God. Or you should serve God through serving men.

So the Lord identifies Himself with those who are in need. Since He is not on earth in bodily form to receive our service to Him, He has made it possible for us to serve Him through those who are the objects of His love.

Like Shakespeare's "quality of mercy," our quality of sharing our blessings "is twice bless'd: it blesses him that gives and him that takes." Thus in sharing your blessings, you multiply them—for yourself and others.

> The paths our bravest ones have trod,
>   O make us brave to go,
> That we may give our lives to God
>   In serving man below;
> So hence shall flow fresh strength and grace
>   As from a full-fed spring,
> And make the world a better place
>   And life a worthier thing.
>
> William DeWitt Howe[1]

---

1. Virginia Ely, *I Quote* (New York: Steward, 1947), pp. 310-11.

# The Joy of Living

*"I am come that they might have life, and that they might have it more abundantly."*—John 10:10b

"Isn't this a great day to be alive!" How often we hear these words. Despite problems, hardships, and heartaches, there are so many blessings that offset them. Truly we can know the joy of living, even though there may be thorns along the way.

Life in its truest sense is more than breathing and moving about. A man said that each morning he rose, ate his breakfast, and then read the obituary column in the newspaper. If he did not find his name listed there, he went back to bed. Such is not living; it is merely existing. Life is purpose, and the nobler the purpose the nobler the life. Jesus said that life is more than food and clothing (Matt. 6:25). In essence it is having something for which to live.

This concept of life was expressed by one who said, "It may be true that I have much less to live on than I had a year ago, but it is certainly true that I have just as much to live for. The real values of life are unshaken and solid. A financial crisis can rob us of all that we have, but it cannot affect what we are."

The Bible speaks of eternal or everlasting life (John 3:16). Life in this sense is not something that begins after death. It is the quality of life which you can know in this earthly sojourn, and which abides in eternity. It was of this "life" that Jesus spoke when He said that He came to give life. And note that He said that you can have it "more abundantly." These words translate one Greek word. It means "overflowing all the edges around." Imagine, if you will, a bucket with one end of a pipe opening into its bottom. The other end is in an inexhaustible, flowing stream. As water flows into the bucket it becomes full to overflowing. And the continous flow continues to overflow. It is that water which overflows that blesses the ground about the bucket.

Really to live you must have this overflowing life. For we bless others by the overflow from our lives. That is what Christ wishes to give to everyone. An anonymous writer has said, "That is what Christianity is for—to teach men the art of Life. And its whole curriculum lies in one word, 'Learn of me.' " Literally, Jesus said, "Learn from me" (Matt. 11:29). His was the most wonderful life ever lived. And He is Life itself (John 14:6). So He both gives you life and teaches you how to live it.

Goethe gives us "Nine requisites for contented living."

> Health enough to make work a pleasure;
> Wealth enough to support your needs;
> Strength to battle with difficulties and overcome them;
> Grace enough to confess sins and forsake them;

> Patience enough to toil until some good is accomplished;
> Charity enough to see some good in your neighbor;
> Love enough to move you to be useful and helpful to others;
> Faith enough to make real the things of God;
> Hope enough to remove all anxious fears concerning the future.

All of these things, and more, are bound up in the more abundant life that Jesus can give to you. Often we hear about someone preparing to die. But you will never be fully prepared to die until first you are prepared to live.

# Pass It On!

*"Freely ye have received, freely give."*—Matt. 10:8

Jesus was sending His twelve apostles on a preaching mission. In effect, He told them to share with others the blessings and power they had received from Him. They had received a gift from God, and were to give it to others. Indeed, if they were to enjoy fully what they had received, they were to pass it on to others. For as Alexandre Dumas said, "We enjoy thoroughly only the pleasures that we give."

The epitaph of Edward Courtenay, Earl of Devonshire, reads:

> What we gave, we have;
> What we spent, we had;
> What we left, we lost.

This is true of money. But it is also true of all of life's blessings.

The bird lives to sing. The flower lives to give off beauty and sweet aroma. And the Christian should live to be a blessing. Indeed, one is never truly blessed until he becomes a blessing.

God does not measure the gift by its quantity, but by its quality and by the love that it expresses. Jesus said that even a cup of cold water given in His name does not lose its reward.

> God, who measures the cup
>   Of mere cold water for His sake
> To a disciple rendered up,
>   Disdains not His own thirst to slake
>     At the poorest love was ever offered.
>
> Robert Browning

Therefore, whatever you have received, pass it on—as generously as you received it. Is it eternal life in Jesus Christ? Pass it on! Is it money? Pass it on! Is it good news? Pass it on! Is it encouragement? Pass it on! Is it sympathetic understanding? Pass it on! Is it forgiveness? Pass it on! Is it love? Pass it on!

For many people the world is such a dreary place. You may not be able to dispel all of its darkness. But you can light one little candle in the name of Christ. And if enough of us do this, we can turn darkness into noonday for some.

Jesus said that you should not put your lamp under a bushel measure. Rather you should put it on a lampstand, that it may give light to all who are about you. Furthermore, He said that a city set on a hill cannot be hid (Matt. 5:14-15). Imagine that you are traveling in the dark—lost. And then suddenly you see a lighted city located on a high place. By it you can get your bearings and find your way to safety.

Christians are to be such beacon lights in the world's darkness.

If a lamp is lighted, it will shine. And if you have God's love in your heart, you must express it to others. Not to call attention to yourself, but to demonstrate the power of God to transform self-centered people into those who center their lives in helping others.

It was this thought which Jesus had in mind when He said, "Let your light so shine before men, that they may see your good works, and glorify your Father which is in heaven" (Matt. 5:16). One act of Christian concern can show God's love more than many sermons. Indeed, if the sermons are not supported by the evidence in one's life, they are not sermons at all.

You may have neither the opportunity nor the talent to proclaim God's love and grace from the pulpit. But you are preaching nevertheless by what you do and say.

So having received freely, give freely. Pass it on! In so doing you will bless another—and be blessed beyond measure in the doing of it.

# Owned or Owner?

*"For the love of money is the root of all evil."*—I Tim. 6:10

Perhaps you have often heard someone say that "money is the root of all evil." This, of course, is not true and is not what the apostle Paul said. There are many evils which are rooted in things other than money.

The fact of the matter is that money properly earned and used may be the root of much good. It is important, therefore, to note exactly what Paul said. Literally, it is "the love of money that is a root of all kinds of evil." "Love of money" renders one Greek word meaning "a love of silver." But the resultant meaning is "a love of money." The Living Bible renders it thus: "For the love of money is the first step toward all kinds of sin." By contrast, the proper regard for money and its use may be the first step toward all kinds of good.

In this dual light the words of an anonymous poet speak volumes to us.

Dug from the mountainside, washed in the glen,
Servant am I, or the master of men;
  Steal me, I curse you,
  Earn me, I bless you,
Grasp me and hoard me, a fiend shall possess you;
Lie for me, die for me, covet me, take me,
Angel or devil, I am what you make me.

# Blessings in Disguise

*"My grace is sufficient for thee: for my strength is made perfect in weakness."*—II Cor. 12:9

In his "Serenades and Songs for a Penthouse Window" Samuel Hoffenstein says, "Blessings love disguise." Which is another way of saying that what outwardly may at the moment seem to be unhappy experiences, are really blessings in disguise when seen in their proper perspective. Doubtless you can recall many such events in your own life.

Paul describes such an experience in II Corinthians 12. He had had a spiritual experience of such nature as to defy description. It might well have produced such inordinate pride in his spirit as to injure his Christian usefulness. But, said he, "there was given to me a thorn in the flesh, the messenger of Satan to buffet me, lest I should be exalted above measure" (v. 7).

What this thorn was he did not say. But it was something designed to humble him. Some see it as some kind of sickness. We simply do not know. But whatever it was, he prayed three times that God would remove it. Instead, God gave him grace to bear it.

Paul learned that what seemed to be an unhappy experience became a blessing in disguise because it taught him to rely on God's strength rather than his own. The Lord said that His grace was enough to suffice for His servant's need. "For my strength is made perfect in weakness." God's power through our weakness is able to fulfil its intended purpose.

In this experience the apostle learned that he must live, not by his own strength, but by God's grace. Too often we think of God's grace only in terms of our redemption. Our forefathers used to speak of God's "enabling grace." And we need to recapture this concept. God saves us by grace, keeps us by grace, and enables us to live the Christian life by grace.

Recall the words of John 1:16: "And of his fulness have all we received, and grace for grace." "Grace for grace" means grace over against grace, or, better still, grace following after grace. At the outset of our lives as Christians God does not give us a ton of grace that must last throughout our lives. "Grace for grace" is like God's gift of manna in the wilderness. The Israelites were not to hoard it, but to gather enough for only one day. A new supply would be given at the start of each new day.

Likewise, God keeps on giving grace, a new supply for every day or testing experience. So when the trial comes, God gives new grace to enable us to bear it.

Said Paul, "Most gladly therefore will I rather glory in my infirmities, that the power of Christ may rest upon me. Therefore I take pleasure in infirmities, in reproaches, in necessities, in persecutions, in distresses for Christ's sake: for when I am weak, then I am strong" (II Cor. 12:9-10).

Recognizing his own weakness, he relied on God's grace; and that made him strong.

He learned through bitter experience what is expressed by the poet:

> Not in rewards, but in the strength to strive,
> The blessing lies.

It is a blessing in disguise, indeed, when we hear God saying, "My grace is sufficient for thee."

# Joy in Tribulation

*"For the same cause also do ye joy, and rejoice with me."*—Phil. 2:18

When he wrote Philippians Paul was a prisoner in Rome. Humanly speaking he had every reason to complain, or as Lum and Abner used to say, to have a case of the "sorrowfuls." But the theme of this letter is "joy." Over and over again the apostle uses the words *joy* and *rejoice*. During the same imprisonment he wrote to the Colossians. In 1:24 he spoke of himself as one "who now rejoices in my sufferings."

The Greek words for *joy* and *rejoice* are akin to the word for *grace*. So your ability to rejoice in tribulation is a gift of God's grace.

We are ever chasing after happiness. But happiness and joy are two different experiences. The very word *happiness* suggests its relation to *happenings*. If things go right you are happy; otherwise, you are unhappy. But joy is a Christian word and emotion. If flows from deep springs within your life, regardless of what may be happening to you on the outside. It was this joy that Jesus experienced even as He endured the cross (Heb. 12:2).

You can know this joy only in a right relationship with Christ. S. D. Gordon said, "It is an unknown world and thing except as He has sway within." So if you would experience joy in hardships, you must first know Jesus Christ as Savior and Lord.

Paul not only had this joy, but he also shared it with others. In Philippians 2:18 "joy" is the simple verb for "joy." But "rejoice" is a compound form of this verb which gives it the force of intensity. His readers rejoiced to know that though he was a prisoner he did well. And he called on them to rejoice the more with him, because despite his present state the gospel continued to be preached by him and others.

As a Christian you can multiply your joy by sharing it with others. Robert Browning said, "Desire joy and thank God for it. Renounce it, if need be, for others' sake. That's joy beyond joy."

No matter what life's circumstances may be for you, you can rejoice in the Lord. To complain and whine over your lot not only discourages others, it also shames the name of Christ who gives you joy. On the other hand, if you let the wellsprings of your inner joy flow, it will bless you and others also.

An anonymous poet has the word for each of us:

> When life seems just a dreary grind,
> And things seem fated to annoy,
> Say something nice to someone else
> And watch the world light up with joy.

# The Blessing of Humility

*"For what maketh thee to differ from another? and what hast thou that thou didst not receive? now if thou didst receive it, why dost thou glory, as if thou hadst not received it?"* —I Cor. 4:7

Someone said that it is all right for a person to be smart or beautiful until he or she finds it out. For having done so, inordinate pride mars the picture.

Such pride produces divisions between men and women. This was true in the Corinthian church as its members centered their loyalty about servants of Christ, rather than about Christ Himself (I Cor. 1:11-13). So Paul reminded them that there should be no grounds for boasting because someone had been won to Christ or had been baptized by a certain person. They were all sinners saved by grace through faith in Christ. So rather than to be boastfully proud before men, they should be humble before God.

This same principle applies in every facet of life. For Paul's question probes our hearts. "What hast thou that thou didst not receive?" No talent, trait, or innate adornment which you have is of your own making. All of these things are gifts from God (I Cor. 12:8-11). A recognition of this truth should result in humility, not pride. Someone said, "The truly godly are instinctively humble. There is no humility so deep and real as that which the knowledge of grace produces." Paul summed it all up when he said, "By the grace of God I am what I am" (I Cor. 15:10).

Of course, you should avoid a false humility. For such is always plainly evident and repugnant to both God and man. Samuel Taylor Coleridge wrote:

> And the Devil did grin, for his darling sin
> Is pride that apes humility.

Uriah Heap was fond of saying that he was a humble man. But it was to cover up his lack of such a virtue. You should never be proud of your humility, but should thank God for His gift of a humble heart.

It has been said that "meekness cannot well be counterfeited. It is not insensibility, or unmanliness, or servility; it does not cringe or whine. It is benevolence imitating Christ in patience, forebearance, and quietness. It feels keenly, but not malignantly; it abounds in good will and bears all things." In like manner Tennyson calls "true Humility the highest virtue, mother of them all."

Inordinate pride is a sign of littleness. It is said that those who parade their virtues seldom lead the procession. But genuine humility is evidence of true greatness. If one is truly great he does not need to throw his weight around. He is considerate of others, especially of those who are not so richly blessed as he is. In the words of Shakespeare, "The eagle suffers little birds to sing."

Genuine humility will be evidenced in your daily conduct.

> Soft is the music that would charm forever;
> The flower of sweetest smell is shy and lowly.
> William Wordsworth

Jesus said, "Whosoever, therefore, shall humble himself as this little child, the same is greatest in the kingdom of heaven" (Matt. 18:4). James said, "God resisteth the proud but giveth grace to the humble" (James 4:6). For this reason you should heed the words of Peter: "Humble yourselves therefore under the mighty hand of God, that he may exalt you in due time" (I Peter 5:6).

# The Virtue of Patience

*"In your patience possess ye your souls."*—Luke 21:19

Jesus was talking to His disciples about the difficulties they would encounter as they sought to serve Him. He promised them protection. But He said more. "In your patience possess ye your souls." The word "possess" means to win or acquire. Some see this to mean that even though they may be killed, through patience they would win life beyond death. But as Christians they already had this assurance; so evidently Jesus meant something else.

To comprehend this meaning you must understand the words rendered "souls" and "patience." The word translated "souls" may mean the principle of life itself. It was also used in the sense of *soul.* But it also meant the purpose for living (Matt. 16:25-26). The context must decide. In Luke 21:19 the sense seems to be the last one.

Unfortunately, the modern popular sense of "patience" is that of simply enduring and waiting through some ordeal or event in anticipation of a blessing. In this sense it is a passive word—and somewhat weak.

But this is not true of the Greek word so rendered. It was an active, courageous word. For instance, it was used of the quality in athletes which enabled them to withstand the opponent, yet possess reserve strength by which to overcome him and win the victory. Also it was used as a military term. Indeed, it was used as a military citation. The Greek papyri reveal a letter from a soldier to his mother telling her that he had been made a *Patient Soldier.* He had been rewarded for bravery in battle. For in this sense it meant that he had withstood the enemy's attack, and possessed reserve strength by which to countercharge to victory. It was most likely that Jesus used the word in this dual sense. By exercising this quality amid persecution they would win the victory over evil and thus fulfil the purpose of their being Christians.

Someone caught this sense of the word when he said, "Patience is not passive; on the contrary, it is active; it is concentrated strength." Thus Paul could say, "We glory in tribulation also; knowing that tribulation worketh [produces] patience" (Rom. 5:3).

Every Christian needs this virtue. By the very strength of body and will you may be able to overcome physical opponents. But to defeat spiritual enemies you need the spiritual quality of *patience.* And such comes only from God. In exile on the isle of Patmos John wrote of having the "patience of Jesus Christ" (Rev. 1:9). The theme of Revelation is the ultimate triumph of Christ and His people.

Jesus never promised that His people would walk a rose scattered path. Rather He said, "In the world ye shall have tribulation [be in a tight place with seemingly no way out]: but be of good cheer [courage]; I have overcome [fully conquered] the world" (John 16:33). In Romans 8 Paul, speaking of the many tight places in which you may find yourself, wrote, "In all these things we are more than conquerors [super-conquerors] through him that loved us" (v. 37).

Doubtless, many who read these words are undergoing great trials. At times you may be tempted to throw in the towel. But remember that Jesus never did; and neither should you. In your own strength alone you may be a loser. But in the patience of Christ which He would give to you, you can win the victory.

Martin Luther's battle hymn of the Reformation puts iron in our blood and steel in our spiritual sinews. Listen to these challenging words:

> A mighty fortress is our God,
> A bulwark never failing;
> Our helper He, amid the flood
> Of mortal ills prevailing. . . .
>
> Did we in our own strength confide,
> Our striving would be losing,
> Were not the right Man on our side,
> The Man of God's own choosing.

And He is on our side! Therefore, "they that wait upon the Lord shall renew their strength; they shall mount up with wings as eagles; they shall run and not be weary, they shall walk and not faint" (Isa. 40:31).

# Contentment

*"I have learned, in whatever state I am, therewith to be content."*—Phil. 4:11

*Contentment* is a beautiful word. Yet to many it is a stranger. Many people live seminomadic lives, never content where they are. The grass is always greener somewhere else. Others eat their hearts out with envy, forever wanting what they do not have but which others possess.

Paul had learned a valuable lesson in life—to be content in whatever state he might be. Actually, the word rendered "content" comes from a verb meaning to be self-sufficient. It means one who governs himself. Not that Paul was independent of others or of God, but rather that God had taught His servant to find peace within himself regardless of outward circumstances.

These words of Paul were written in response to a gift (probably money) from his friends in Philippi. So he recognized the help that they had rendered to him. He was grateful. But even had they not sent it, he would have been content in his lot; for he had learned the secret of living with much or little (Phil. 4:12). He had learned the truth in Socrates' words. When asked who is the wealthiest person, the great philosopher replied, "He that is content with least, for *autarkeia* [contentment] is nature's wealth."

Now Paul was not content with what he *was*. For in this same letter he said, "Not as though I had already attained, either were already perfect: but I follow after [press on], if that I may apprehend that for which also I am apprehended of Christ Jesus. Brethren, I count not myself to have apprehended: but this one thing I do, forgetting those things which are behind, and reaching forth unto those things which are before, I press toward the mark of the prize of the high calling of God in Christ Jesus" (3:12-14).

He wanted to lay hold on the full purpose for which Christ had laid hold on him. As a runner in a race, he forgot past failures and successes in order to run successfully the race in which he now found himself. Like a runner, he stretched forth to achieve the prize of victory in Christian living. He knew by experience the truth spoken by another: "It is right to be contented with what we have, never with what we are."

Paul's contentment lay in what he had. Though a prisoner in Rome he found a self-sufficiency in Christ to endure hardship and want (Phil. 4:13). Like Whittier the poet, he said:

> No longer forward nor behind
> I look in hope or fear;
> But grateful, take the good I find
> The best of now and here.

William Temple, the British theologian, said that "contentment with the divine will is the best remedy we can apply to misfortune." You may not always understand, but you can trust your heavenly Father. And in His own time He will make all things plain.

Writing to Timothy, Paul said, "But godliness with contentment is great gain. For we brought nothing into this world, and it is certain that we can carry nothing out. And having food and raiment let us be therewith content" (I Tim. 6:6-8).

"Godliness with contentment." This should be the goal of each one of us. And achieving both is a double blessing indeed. You can do this as

> Without murmur, uncomplaining,
>   In His hand,
> Leave whatever things thou canst not
>   Understand.
>
> K. R. Hagenbach

# Faith

*"Faith is the substance of things hoped for; the evidence of things not seen."*—Heb. 11:1

> I will not doubt though all my ships at sea
>   Come drifting home with broken masts and sails;
>   I will believe the Hand that never fails
> From seeming evil worketh good for me,
> And though I weep because those sails are tattered,
> Still will I cry, while my best hopes lie shattered—
>   "I trust in Thee."
>
>                                     Ella Wheeler Wilcox

In beautiful words the poet has expressed the essence of Hebrews 11:1. Indeed, she embraces all of Hebrews 11, a chapter sometimes referred to as the "Westminster Abbey of the Bible."

Actually, "faith is the assurance [guarantee] of things hoped for; the conviction [proof] of things not seen." I like the paraphrase of this verse in The Living Bible. "What is Faith? It is the confident assurance that something we want is going to happen. It is the certainty that what we hope for is waiting for us, even though we cannot see it up ahead."

Some people feel that faith belongs to the realm of the unreal like the little girl who said that faith is believing something that you know is not so. But in Hebrews 11:1 "things" renders a word from which comes our word *pragmatic*. So faith is pragmatic; it works! As one has said, "Faith is the daring of the soul to go farther than it can see." Where reason must stop, faith takes a daring leap into the unknown. It is thus that the unknown becomes the known.

Every worthy human enterprise begins as an act of faith. In faith that the world was round, not flat, Columbus sailed *west* to go *east*. And he discovered a new world. Those who have a disposition to believe are constantly discovering new worlds. The research scientist begins a project in faith. He believes that there is something he does not know, but that he can discover it by following certain fixed laws of the Lawgiver. In such faith science has given us the wonders of the modern age.

Faith is the element that holds life together. Without faith there could be no family, government, or social order. Without faith we would live in a chaos, not in a cosmos.

Of course, faith in its richest form is religious faith.

> Faith is a grasping of Almighty power;
>   The hand of man laid on the arm of God;
> The grand and blessed hour
> In which the things impossible to me
> Become the possible, O Lord, through Thee.

And faith in its purest essence is Christian faith. Such faith surmounts legalism and guilt to find forgiveness in Jesus

Christ. And it ventures forth for Him despite difficulties and discouragements. Nathaniel Hawthorne once wrote, "Christian faith is a grand cathedral, with divinely pictured windows. Standing without you see no glory, nor can imagine any. But standing within every ray of light reveals a harmony of unspeakable splendors."

Men without faith are as toads sitting in the mud. But men of faith are as eagles soaring above the commonplace and seemingly impossible to view the vast vistas of God's grace, love, and power. As one has said, cynicism and fear freeze life; but faith thaws it out, releases it, and sets it free. Reason is puzzled by the mystery, but faith cuts the Gordian knot and out of its threads weaves a tapestry of beauty and usefulness.

It should be remembered, however, that faith is not passive but active. Jesus said, "If ye have faith as a grain of mustard seed, ye shall say unto this mountain [Mount Hermon, Palestine's tallest mountain], Remove hence to yonder place; and it shall remove; and nothing shall be impossible to you" (Matt. 17:20).

Note that Jesus did not say "as big as a mustard seed" but "as a mustard seed." He spoke of quality, not quantity. Faith has in it the quality of life which works to achieve its goal. Plant a grain of mustard seed in the earth. It will germinate and grow. Place a clod of dirt on it. If it cannot grow through it, it will grow around it. A faith that can move mountains will use a shovel, if necessary, to accomplish its purpose.

At times faith may seem to go unrewarded. It is then that you need the faith of patience to wait on God. He works by *His* timetable, not yours. And in His own time and way faith will receive its reward.

Unanswered yet? Faith cannot be unanswered.
Her feet are firmly planted on the Rock;
Amid the wildest storms she stands undaunted
Nor quails before the loudest thunder shock.
She knows Omnipotence has heard her prayer
And cries, "It shall be done, sometime, somewhere."

# Hope

*"Now the God of all hope fill you with all joy and peace in believing, that ye may abound in hope, through the power of the Holy Ghost [Spirit]."*—Rom. 15:13

What would life be without hope? It would be nothing more than a den of despair. But hope, like angels' wings, lifts us up, lest we dash our feet on the stones of doubt and disillusionment.

Paul reminds us that hope finds its source in God and is given to us through the Holy Spirit. And, of course, such hope is available only to those who have a saving relation with God through Jesus Christ (II Thess. 2:16). Leslie D. Weatherhead reminds us that when the psalmist wrote, "Hope thou in God," he gave us the only basis of hope there is.

Hope is the earnest expectation that what good you have not experienced or received is real, and in time will become your own. Even in the darkest night hope tells us that " 'Tis always morning somewhere" (Longfellow). It is, indeed, the morning star that heralds the coming dawn.

> Hope, like the gleaming taper's light
>   Adorns and cheers our way;
> And still, as darker grows the night
>   Emits a brighter ray.
>
> Oliver Goldsmith

Hope not only lights the darkened way, it also enables the traveler to look up and see the beckoning and assuring hand of God. As the dark comes, so will it be followed by the sunrise. And each sunrise gives promise of a new day, new opportunities, new realizations.

Note, however, that the psalmist three times said, "Hope thou in God" (42:5, 11; 43:5). Hope that is mere wishful thinking is but a will-o'-the-wisp. For hope to be well founded it must be in God.

> O safe to the Rock that is higher than I,
> My soul in its conflicts and sorrows
>   would fly;
> So sinful, so weary, Thine own would I be;
> Thou blest "Rock of Ages," I'm hiding
>   In Thee.
>
> William O. Cushing

Our hope in God rests in His strength, not our own. Men may fail us, but God never does. And hope based on faith in Christ looks not to that which is, but to that which will be. Titus 2:13-14 exhorts us to be "looking for that blessed hope, and the glorious appearing of the great God and [even] our Savior Jesus Christ; who gave himself for us, that he might redeem us from all iniquity, and purify unto himself a peculiar people, zealous of good works."

Your hopes may not be realized in this life. But the Christian knows that all that is worthy of eternal values will be received when Christ comes to right all wrongs and to give us in full blossom those things which now bud in our hearts.

> Ne'er was the sky so deep a blue
> But that the sun comes breaking through;
> There never was a night so dark
> But wakened to the singing lark;
> Nor was there a lane so long
> It had no turn for the weary throng,
> Nor heart so sad that sometime after
> There came no sound or lilting laughter;
> And death's not the end 'neath the cold
>   black sod—
> 'Tis the inn by the road on the way to God.
> 
> Charles Dudley Warner

# Love

*"And now abideth faith, hope, love, these three; but the greatest of these is love."*—I Cor. 13:13

The popular idea is to see I Corinthians as Paul's "Ode to Love." However, rather than this it is the basic part or heart of his argument in showing Christians how to live with each other (I Cor. 12–14). So instead of being simply a rhapsody of poetic beauty, it is the hard core of reason as to the place that love should have in personal relationships (see I Cor. 12:31–13:13).

Unfortunately, the English word *love* is extremely vague in meaning. It is used all the way from sexual attraction, to loving apple pie, to loving a friend, to loving God. The Greek language is not so vague, for it has different words to express various kinds of love. *Eros* was used for sexual, sensual attraction. (Note our word *erotic*.) *Philia* was used for the love of warm friendship. *Agape* was the highest kind of love, whose basic meaning is absolute loyalty to its object. It was this word used by John when he said, "God is love" (I John 4:8). And it is the word used by Paul in I Corinthians 13.

Unfortunately, the King James Version translates it "charity." This word has an entirely different meaning today.

This *agape* love has its source in the very nature of God. It is His love to man (I John 4:10). Through faith in Christ believers return this love to God. And in Christ it is the Christian's love toward all men, especially those of the household of faith.

Paul says that this love should qualify every deed of the Christian (I Cor. 13:1-3). It should characterize his every attitude (vv. 4-7). It is the gift of the Holy Spirit above all other gifts. Other gifts (prophecy, tongues, knowledge) may be temporary or pass away. But love is the abiding gift which characterizes the adult Christian and enables him to know God as he is known of Him (vv. 8-12).

Not only is Christian love a gift from God, it should be the seasoning which makes wholesome and delightful the life of the Christian. Because God is love, we should love. Indeed, if we say that we love God yet do not love our Christian brother, we are living a lie (I John 4:11, 20). The Christian should love all people. God loves us not because of what we are, but in spite of what we are (Rom. 5:6-8). You do not have to agree with a person, or even *like* him as an individual, to show Christian love toward him. But since all men are made in God's image and endowed with the dignity of human personality—and since God loves them—so should you love them.

William Wordsworth wrote:

> Mightier far
> Than strength of nerve and sinew, or
>   the sway
> Of magic potent over sun and star
>   Is love.

Thus love in your heart will enable you to rise above human problems and differences to show love to your fellowmen. To know that God loves us in spite of ourselves should lead us to love others the same way. And loving others, we will in turn be loved by them.

Rosalie Mills Appleby is known for the beauty of her life and her service to others. Awareness of this dedication enhances her words when she says, "Love is the dove of peace that soars out on the wings of the morning to greater spiritual heights. It is the angel's flight to a higher world of beauty, lifting life from its dust to meet the sunrise of God. It is beauty incarnated, kindness glorified, and goodness sanctified."

Love enables us to rise above ourselves, to overcome our pettiness, to become courageous and noble. But as someone said, "It is a sacred fire that must not be burned to idols." It may cost you pain to love. But in the words of Sir Walter Scott, "Love is loveliest when embalm'd in tears." Even bereavement is the price that we pay for love. But the dividends of love far outweigh the losses it entails. And when our life on earth is ended, we will be more at home in heaven because we have loved.

> Love is the filling from one's own
>   Another's cup;
> Love is the daily laying down
>   And taking up;
> A choosing of the stony path
>   Through each new day
> That other feet may tread with ease
>   A smoother way.
> Love is not blind, but looks abroad
>   Through other eyes;

And asks not, "Must I give?" but
  "May I sacrifice?"
Love hides its grief, that other hearts
  And lips may sing;
And burdened walks, that other lives
  May buoyant wing.
Hast thou a love like this
  Within thy soul?
'Twill crown thy life with bliss
  When thou dost reach the goal.

# Growing Lovely, Growing Old

*"And thine age shall be clearer than the noonday; thou shalt shine forth, thou shalt be as the morning."*—Job 11:17

Many years ago I recall a chapel message brought by John R. Sampey, retired president of Southern Baptist Theological Seminary. He spoke of the fact that he was growing old. Said he, "As an apple ages it will either mellow or rot. I hope that I can mellow."

Which speaks of the blessings of old age. You can either *rot,* and become a burden to yourself and others, or you can *mellow,* and be a blessing to the same. Someone said that "the evening of a well-spent life brings its lamps with it." Such a person can truly say with Robert Browning:

> Grow old along with me!
> The best is yet to be,
> The last of life, for which the first was made.
> Our times are in His hand,
> Who saith: "A whole life I planned,
> Youth shows but half; trust God; see all, nor be afraid."

We often speak of the beauty of childhood. But there can also be a lovely old age touched with the multicolored rays of a setting sun. The passing of the years may put wrinkles on your brow but they need not be in your heart. The real you is your spirit. And it should never grow old. Tryon Edwards says, "Age does not depend upon years, but upon temperament and health. Some men are born old and some never grow old."

So one may be old in spirit even though young in years. Anyone who has lost his dreams or the forward look is old. If you become self-satisfied and cease the upward climb, then you are old—no matter what the calendar says.

But so long as you keep your dreams, follow your visions, retain your sense of humor, and continue to love, you will never really become old. Your hair may turn white; but by your sparkling zest for life, as one has said, you can be a living reminder that those parts of earth—and life—are whitest which are nearest to heaven.

You should make the poet's prayer your prayer:

> Let me grow lovely growing old,
>   So many fine things to do;
> Laces, ivory, and gold,
>   And silks need not be new.
> There is healing in old trees,
>   Old streets a glamor hold
> Why not I, as well as these
>   Grow lovely growing old?
>
> Karle Wilson Baker